Turbulence

Turbulence

Climate change and
the design of complexity

Paul Carter

PUNCHER & WATTMANN

First published in 2015
Published by Puncher and Wattmann
PO Box 441
Glebe NSW 2037
http://www.puncherandwattmann.com
puncherandwattmann@bigpond.com

National Library of Australia
Cataloguing-in-Publication entry

Carter, Paul
Turbulence

ISBN 978-1-922186-79-9
I. Title.
A821.3

Cover design by Matthew Holt
Printed by McPhersons Printing Group

This project has been assisted by the Australian Government through the Australia
Council, its arts funding and advisory body; and the University of Technology Sydney.

Let me offer you a myth.
Gregory Bateson[1]

Involute 1, artline texta 0.4 on paper, 210 x 297 mm, March 2014. Source: Paul Carter, Australian Notebook (hereafter A) A46a, 31.

Foreword

In the text that follows Paul Carter positions the idea of turbulence as a means by which to understand multi-factorial complex change. He suggests turbulence does not have a single meaning, placing it in relationship to cultural shifts, scientific endeavour, political economy and importantly, a consideration of design.

Climate change and the design of complexity also describes an interdisciplinary project. It acts as a diary of sorts – a documentation if you like of various 'thought-paths' of iterations of the project. While turbulence is introduced as a way to respond to climate change, at its heart lies the broader philosophical proposition of turbulence as a concept to navigate and explicate complexity. It also maps Carter's ongoing interests in the politics and poetics of space, place making, the dramaturgy and choreography of encounter, the constitution and formation of public space, the importance of sense-making to meaning and 'dark writing.'

Professor Paul Carter was a Distinguished Visiting Scholar in the Faculty of Design, Architecture and Building, University of Technology Sydney in 2013. The Centre for Contemporary Design Practices (CCDP) hosted his visit. An initial sketch of his concept was presented to the Faculty in October 2012 as part of his keynote lecture: 'Material Gestures: political economy of creative research,' and developed further during his residency in 2013 under the banner of Turbulence.

Turbulence was presented as a way to consider and encourage discussions around interdisciplinary research. Participants were invited to think differently about their research, its disciplinary boundaries and its social function. Interrogating what Carter terms a 'forming situation,' the project initiated a series of provocations, not the least being the challenge of 'translating' between disciplines and a consideration of the idea of transformative change in relation to the context of the university as an institutionalized space of public knowledge production. The question of how design might be located within the research context of the university was also raised. As Carter makes the point, 'Turbulence is not simply a complex and unpredictable cultural or physical environment... it is the self-conscious awareness of the power of feedback mechanisms to inaugurate new behaviours.' As such, the project provided a discursive opening for a deeper consideration of the role of the researcher and the place and space of research.

It was a great privilege to work closely with Paul over a period of several months. We would like to thank Paul firstly for his interest in participating in the Distinguished Visiting Scholar scheme and for his generous engagement with researchers in the Faculty through the Centre for Contemporary Design Practices. We would also like to thank him for the incisiveness and discernment that he brought to the many and various discussions convened during his residency. Early Career Researchers especially benefitted from both his expert knowledge and depth of research experience. His insights had a generative effect for many and continue to inspire.

Lastly, we wish to thank David Musgrave and Matthew Holt from Puncher & Wattmann for their support and interest in bringing this project to publication.

Benedict Anderson
Director
Bronwyn Clark-Coolee
Manager

Centre for Contemporary Design Practices
University of Technology Sydney

Preface

The formalization of design as a distinctive methodology for the solution of real world problems has raised questions about its status as a mode of knowledge. The unity of design as a field of theory and practice remains in doubt: in certain traditional specializations, design is indistinguishable from functionality. Even when functionality is redefined in terms of soft, affective responses, design appears to lack the independence of art. In other forums, notably in architectural design, both functionality and formalism fall away and new kinds of algorithmically informed pattern-making have at best a tangential relationship to our perceived needs. Aside from these issues of identity and purpose, design suffers – at least in the rhetorically driven university – from its dumbness. Much can be, and has been, made of the metaphorical fertility of drawing – of 'drawing out' and 'drawing in' as social practices – but design remains subservient to the fulfilment of externally determined interests (the brief). Even the much vaunted difference of design education – the iterative procedures of the design studio – drives towards some practical resolution of a real world problem.

One symptom of design's hybrid reformation in the academy, where it belongs equally to fashion, the aerospace industries, the alliance with nano-technology and, for example, new 'flow world' thinking[2] is its attractiveness to non-specialists, including practical philosophers who perceive in its obstinate commitment to materialization a robust vehicle for a new anti-metaphysicalist praxis of everyday life. The emphasis on process, the drive towards the production of objects, equipment or assemblages that fit together, the extension of the line of design to embrace the logic of the gesture the surrounding ambience of the work and the reciprocity (or good object relations) that design solicits, make it a richly

---

1   Gregory Bateson, *Steps to an Ecology of Mind* (Chicago: University of Chicago Press, 2000), 440.
2   Nigel Thrift, 'Movement-space: The Changing Domain of Thinking Resulting from the Development of New Kinds of Spatial Awareness,' *Economy & Society* 33, 4 (2004): 582-604, 590.

suggestive medium of testing ideas. Good ideas will not be measured by their theoretical coherence but by their capacity to inform constructions that possess utility. Philosophers and artists have always collaborated – a notable recent example being the exchanges between Chillida and Heidegger[3] – and, I suppose, the new pretension of design to offer a distinctive mode of real world analysis is also finding its place in professional and scholarly discourse.

Against this background *Turbulence* reports on a recent experiment to discover what unity design might possess amid the myriad specialist expressions and meanings it has traditionally possessed. Recognizing design's weakness as a disciplinary formation, a group of us at the University of Technology Sydney (UTS) considered the promiscuity of design as a research practice as offering a propitious medium for cross-disciplinary communication. In particular, the suspension of design between language and image might, we thought, offer a tool for suspending differences long enough to find improvised common ground. Somewhere between drawing and speaking, an iterative process of problem identification might allow certain foreclosures of brief, institutional expectation and methodological resource to emerge. In particular, the nature of complexity interested us: could a pluralistic adaptation of different design methods usefully bring into question the identification of the successful research program with the reduction of complexity to simplicity? The paradox of publicly funded research programs that purport to solve 'wicked problems' (that is, complex real world inequities, deficiencies or other multifactorial threats to collective well-being) by proposing simple solutions is well known. Yet the prejudice against descriptions that participate in complexity through its mimetic

---

3   Usefully discussed by Marcia Brennan, *Curating Consciousness: Mysticism and the Modern Museum* (Cambridge, Mass.: The MIT Press, 2010), 195-198. Heidegger's fascination with Chillida's work relates directly to its materialisation of turbulence: the sculpture as *topos* collapses the distinction between outside and inside, emptiness and plenitude. The new 'volume' is the gesture of place-seeking and place-forming.

reformulation – drawing it out – remains firmly embedded in the scientistic criteria used to decide the allocation of research funding.

A new narrative is needed if complexity is to be communicated in terms that respect its sublimity. The proposition is that the figurative fertility of design, its hybrid combination of graphic abstraction and concrete materialization, captures something of the feedback between ideation and environment that is the genuine analogue of complexity. Design is, like geography, amorphous as a research field, sometimes awkwardly suspended between spatial or topological literalism and the representation of volumetric or durational processes that cannot be otherwise modeled or visualized. Just as scientific theory often resorts to spatial metaphors to explain logical relations, so design easily mistakes the model for a mode of conceptualization that can shape thought, rather than embodying preconceived instructions. To bring focus to our experiment, without at the same time predetermining the scope of the enquiry, I suggested that our theme, the apprehensible phenomenon that we could all recognize, might be 'turbulence.'

Further, to contextualize our discussions, I suggested we use the case study of 'Hamlet's Mill,' an ongoing research project to develop armatures capable of communicating the character of climate change. In *Material Thinking* a distinguishing feature of creative research is said to be its response to a 'forming situation.'[4] In its crudest sense a 'forming situation' is a plan for change. It can cover any intervention in the public realm that involves a modification of human behavior. The 'forming situation' to which 'Hamlet's Mill' responded was the Greater London Council's resolve to assume global leadership in climate change education. This was an opportunity to evaluate existing public education models – and, we argued, to place creative research at the heart of the strategy. Creative research mediates between memory, imagination and invention, and, we

---

4   Paul Carter, *Material Thinking: The Theory and Practice of Creative Research* (Carlton, Vic: Melbourne University Publishing, 2004), 15.

proposed, cultural innovation should therefore be tied to cultural memory. In this context we revived an ancient association of Shakespeare's anti-hero, Hamlet, with the 'turner of the world,' a mythical figure associated with the introduction of turbulence into the order of things.[5]

There is, as we quickly found out, turbulence at the heart of design, for the hydrologist's response to the problem of managing turbulent flow turns out to be markedly different from that of the urban designer intrigued to incubate richer forms of sociability. We could not resolve such differences of taste and purpose but the conversations that resulted throw light on the expanded role design might play in a reformed research ecology, one where the old stand-off between narrative explanations and axiom-driven accounts of nature yields to a definition of useful knowledge predicated on the 'sense' of things. Such a reformation of the arts/science divide is not simply a shifting of the deckchairs on a sinking funding model: it embodies a radical reappraisal of the relationship between the research sector and what have hitherto been called 'industry partners.' The old public/private interest criterion of knowledge production and innovation eliminates from active participation the dominant middle ground of the creative community, which reaches out in both directions, towards the forming situation and the governance principles that apply to its care and design. After citizen science there is an urgent need to foster citizen design, where the mediation of different interests, positions and histories produces patterns of complexity rather than over-simplification. Such patterns enable processes of change, transformation and growth to be visualized, evaluated and guided. They correspond to a new kind of pedagogy and a public space whose production is continuous.

---

5   Our reference text was Giorgio de Santillana and Hertha von Dechend's quirky but sometimes brilliantly speculative study *Hamlet's Mill: An Essay Investigating the Origins of Human Knowledge and its Transmission Through Myth* (Jaffrey, New Hampshire: David R. Godine Publisher Inc., 1977).

1. Introduction

In *The Postmodern Condition*, Lyotard uses the criterion of performativity to account for the overthrow of the 'grand narratives' that had formerly driven the search for knowledge. With the advent of computerization, itself an intensification of the knowledge-as-information paradigm, what matters more than ever is not whether a statement or hypothesis is 'true' but whether what results from it works (performs). Technological innovation is 'proof' that the performativity criterion works.[6] Lyotard further suggests that performativity is associated with consensus forming. It provides the tacit criterion of truth in an 'interdisciplinary approach... specific to the age of delegitimation and its hurried empiricism.'[7] The internalization of the truth criteria produces an institutionalized knowledge that strengthens its own operability at the expense of a connection to the real world. Teamwork may be 'successful in improving performativity within the framework of a given model,' but it is less useful when 'the need is to "imagine".'[8] This foreclosure on the radically new represents a crisis, which Lyotard's 'postmodern science' seeks to address. Given that the 'modern' constantly jettisons 'models,' constantly announcing the new, there must exist an interstitial period of instability when the new model is struggling to displace the old one. The 'postmodern,' Lyotard argues, locates itself in this terrain and is characterized by a '*paralogism*, in which the point is not to reach agreement but to undermine from within the very framework in which the previous "normal science" had been conducted.'[9]

Lyotard borrows his notion of performativity from J.L. Austin, but the result of defining performativity as a form of context control is to leach

---

6   Jean-François Lyotard, *The Postmodern Condition: A Report on Knowledge*, trans. Geoffrey Bennington and Brian Massumi (Manchester: Manchester University Press, 1984), 46.

7   Ibid., 52.

8   Ibid., 52.

9   Fredric Jameson, 'Foreword,' *The Postmodern Condition*, xix.

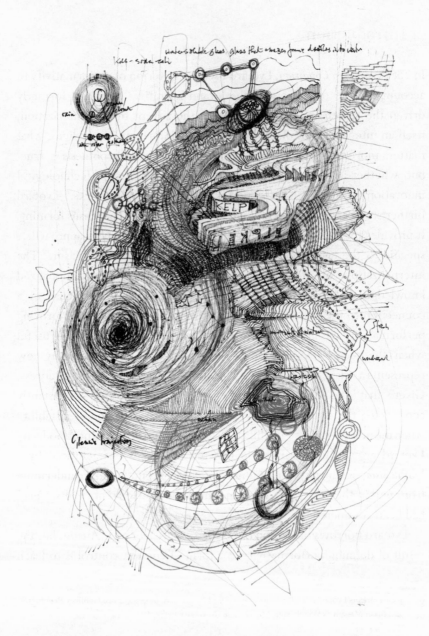

Involute 2, artline texta 0.4 on paper, 210 x 297 mm, July 2014. A46a, 101.

8

out what might be described as the distinctively performative dimension of performance. What Lyotard says about performativity could be applied equally to any kind of rule-bound language game, where the players collude to maintain the consensus (the rules of the game). However, 'the little narrative' that 'remains the quintessential form of imaginative invention,'[10] is also performative: 'differential or imaginative or paralogical activity'[11] intervenes, contradicts and, above all, displays the heteromorphous nature of knowledge.[12] There is no reason why a 'team' engaging in this kind of 'postmodern science' should achieve consensus. On the contrary, after the breakdown of the *grands récits* that once provided common ground, it is more likely that specializations will simply agree to disagree. It would require particular circumstances or a 'crisis' to induce institutionalized researchers to participate in the kind of 'language game' played out, for example, in the *Parmenides*, where, instead of consensus, the incommensurability of viewpoints becomes itself the knowledge the occasion bestows.[13]

This is the context in which in 2014, visiting the design research community at the University of Technology Sydney, I proposed a new kind of research dialogue. One novelty of this was to locate design in the spectrum of knowledge discourses. Although Lyotard is in other contexts a prominent advocate of the postmodern in art, characterizing it as work that 'puts forward the unpresentable in presentation itself,'[14] his knowledge taxonomy in *The Postmodern Condition* remains traditionally binary, a contest between non-narrative (science) and narrative (philosophy) forms of conceptualization. However, particularly with the advent of computer aided design, design comes to occupy a hybrid position in the knowledge

---

10   Lyotard, *Postmodern Condition*, 62.

11   Ibid., 65.

12   Ibid., 66.

13   See Paul Carter, *Dark Writing: Geography, Performance, Design* (Honolulu: Hawa'ii University Press, 2008), 95-96.

14   Lyotard, *Postmodern Condition*, 81.

hierarchy, mediating between a new performativity available to it through parametric modeling and a continuing qualitative engagement with the entire field of sense-making which, in design, focuses on the challenge of better place-making. Technically, as well as philosophically, it enjoys certain advantages as a mediator in any 'interdisciplinary' project. While it may be unable to build consensus, it is able to visualize problems at different scales and in situation and contexts that specialists from a range of disciplines can immediately recognize as relevant to their concerns.

The particular provocation proposed was the representation of complexity. It is an oddity of Lyotard's survey that, while he welcomes science's post-positivist development of a non-representationalist model of scientific knowledge, he does not consider the possibility of a post-disciplinary research program, one in which the 'instabilities' he takes to be symptomatic of conceptual innovation serve themselves as objects of study. His focus on the ways knowledge is legitimized may explain this: in the institution, power is identified with simplification; performativity goes together with efficiency, and both imply the elimination of risk-taking or speculation. Here, at least, Lyotard's thirty year old analysis of the Canadian situation remains valid in Australia. More than ever, researchers are under pressure to perform; the competitiveness of research proposals is decided by a consensus likely to reward those who refine the efficiency of the present model rather than those who question it. It is in the interest of the institution to maintain the state where 'there are some things that should not be said.'[15] Above all, it is not in the interests of the universities to support research that seeks to complexify. There will be many reasons why, for example, an interdisciplinary, or even post-disciplinary, approach to understanding the nature and implications of climate challenge will fail - the feedback loop between public policy development (and planning generally) and the kinds of research program that are valorized and supported is well-known, but there is also the

---

15   Ibid., 17.

challenge of performativity. How, that is, will complexity be visualized, a model developed that puts forward the unpresentable in the presentation itself? The conundrum is analogous to the construction of a *controlled* experiment to study the behavior of turbulence.

As a form of material thinking, design research flourishes best in response to a 'forming situation.' However, a 'forming situation' is not just a top-down decision for change. It also occurs wherever planned or proposed change meets resistance. Self-organizing systems, human and nonhuman, are characteristically homeostatic. They exhibit what might be called an ecological aesthetic, the sum of the interactions tending to maintain the stability of the whole. In contrast, the ideology of planned progress assumes the muteness of matter (human and non-human) and proceeds with all the hubris of the Creator to give what it takes to be formless desirable shape. Historically, there is a self-reinforcing relationship between the emergence of systems theory in response to the non-workability of linear descriptions of complex change and the impoverishment of our capacity to think about change differently. Where change is either catastrophic or tends to cancel out all trace of the former situation, the design of change remains in the hands of the expert. In a forming situation of immediate interest to designers – the on-going 'revitalization' of public space – the conflict is immediately apparent: the planners' rhetorical commitment to place-making invariably aims to filter out any remnant of community self-organization. The designer's intervention can be characterized as a late attempt to preserve the illusion of openness and growth, and often appears as little more than the respectable face of another experiment in social engineering.

Design research that avoided this collusionist fate would need to define its own forming situations and convene its own real-world laboratories. Originally, as mentioned, the impulse to promote a new arts/sciences dialogue around the representation of complexity had focused on a proposal to create a climate change monitor. 'Hamlet's Mill,' originally mooted in 2007, took the phenomenon of climate change skepticism as its site of real world resistance. Our thesis was that differences of view about the existence, causes and implications of global climate change could not be resolved within the present representationalist frameworks. In an effort to visualize complex change, the debate had spiraled down into over-simplifications that impoverished, rather than expanded, our capacity for care. The role of design in this context was not simply to bridge the gap between quantitative and qualitative – between data sets and information – more effectively: it was to show the nexus between change and public space. In its classic democratic definition public space is where political change is negotiated. It was within the capacity of design to show us that the debate about climate change concealed something deeper – the ontological claim of democracy to secure the grounds of coexistence. In other words, the climate change monitor was public space as such when it was retrieved, or designed, for the common good.

'Hamlet's Mill' contained the seeds of a research program. However, within the region it proposed to explore the areas that could be planned were small. A certain amount of progress could be made in locating appropriate environmental monitoring data sets, and limited precedents for their artistic interpretation existed. However, the goal was not aesthetic but educative, in the primary sense of leading people out into a new, shared place of democratic agency over the design of public space, where, for example, the phenomenon of change could be shown to obey certain feedback principles tending to more complex forms of communication and social organization. To organize this possibility, it was necessary to engage creative communities, political leaders, educational and cultural institutions. A promising step in this direction occurs in 'Governing Civilization through Civilizing Governance: Global challenge for a turbulent future,' prepared by the Global Governance School of the New School of Athens (2008), which perspicaciously captures the current stand-off between prevailing 'myths' of governance and civil society and proposes steps for dismantling them. In particular, it urges respect for 'craziness' as a symptom of an emergent reality that defies linear, hierarchical thinking, embracing instead a transition to a new order of complexity and self-organization.[16]

The task of reframing governance involves 'designing in challenging feedback loops,' 'necessarily self-reflexive fractal framing' so that the new '(non) model' is continually open to challenge. A governance system that is cognitively equipped to respond to the 'emergent reality' can 'evoke competence, insight and creative engagement wherever it is to be found'[17] and it supports 'realistic concern to focus on higher order complementary opportunities.'[18] Finally, and refreshingly, it emphasizes the importance of reversing our present 'metaphorical impoverishment' in order to be able to think concretely and creatively in new ways about governance and globalization.[19] The concrete expression of these aspirations in design practice would be a choreotopography focused on the dramaturgy of encounter.[20]

It became apparent in this context that the challenge of visualizing complexity has its organizational counterpart in the goals, mindsets, specializations and operational regimes of the authorities charged to administer the services expected by the community. Of note were the obstacles to the integration of different kinds of knowledge offered by the universities. Research programs conducted across the arts and sciences typically study phenomena that present complex features and invite nuanced interpretation, but the larger question of the commensurability of different fields of investigation is avoided. Intensification and refinement are supported on the grounds they may produce technicist advantage; the larger fragmentation of research fields and the growing irrelevance of such research in the quest to understand and design our collective destiny is obvious.

---

16   'Governing Civilization through Civilizing Governance: Global challenge for a turbulent future.' Accessed at www.laetusinpraesens.org/pdfs/civilgov.pdf.

17   Ibid.

18   Ibid.

19   Ibid.

20   See Paul Carter, *Places Made After Their Stories: Design and the Art of Choreotopography* Nedlands, WA: University of Western Australia Publishing, 2015.

The object of these notes is to take seriously the materialization of such resistances to change. *Turbulence* is in this sense the diary of the turbulence encountered when new fields and models of research are proposed. The philosopher John Dewey remarked, 'The union of the hazardous and the stable, of the incomplete and the recurrent, is the condition of all experienced satisfaction as truly as of our predicaments and problems... For if there were nothing in the way... no deviations and resistances, fulfillment would be at once, and... would fulfill nothing, merely be. It would not be in connection with desire or satisfaction.'[21] The conundrum of designing procedures for the kind of research 'Hamlet's Mill' proposed may be said to have humanized the original research question. The design of public space became inseparable from understanding the present governance structures shaping, limiting and directing research. The turbulence of complex change could not be separated from the complex forces arrayed institutionally to repress the turbulence associated with complex change.

2. Turbulence

To visualize complexity demands a prior conceptualization of the phenomenon:

> Observe the motion of the surface of the water, which resembles that of hair, which has two motions, of which one is caused by the weight of the hair, the other by the direction of the curls; thus the water has eddying motions, one part of which is due to the principal current, the other to random and reverse motion.

---

21   John Dewey, *The Later Works of John Dewey, Volume 1: 1925, Experience and Nature* (Illinois: Southern Illinois Press, 1981), 57.

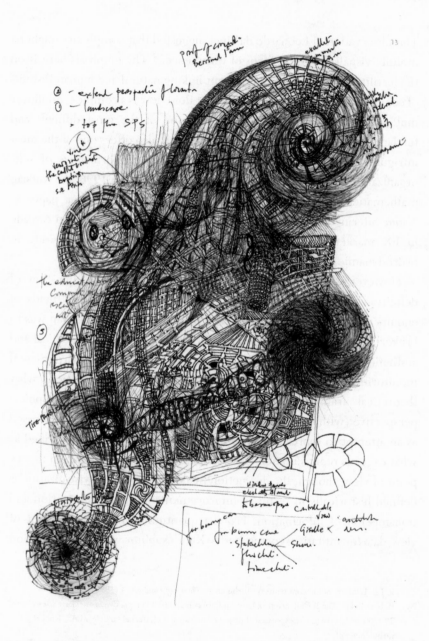

Involute 3, artline texta 0.4 on paper. 210 x 297 mm, August 2013. A46, 33.

15

This observation of Leonardo da Vinci suggested that complexity might be usefully visualized in the form of turbulence.[22] The emphasis here is on the fertility of turbulence as a concept linking natural and human systems of complex self-organization. 'Turbulent fluid flow is a complex, nonlinear multiscale phenomenon, which poses some of the most difficult and fundamental problems in classical physics.'[23] It also offers one of the most intriguing signs that genuine common, underlying principles of self-organization may exist in natural and human systems. In 1996, the Russian mathematician and scientist Andrei Kolmogorov published a paper in *Nature* offering impressive evidence that 'there is an information cascade in FX market dynamics that corresponds to the energy cascade in hydrodynamic turbulence.'[24]

However, this suggestive correspondence begged the question of definition: had turbulence the same connotation in different fields of enquiry? If, following the lead offered by 'Hamlet's Mill,' the plan was to broker a new arts/sciences dialogue focused on the technical, ethical and aesthetic challenges of taking large data sets derived from environmental monitoring stations and turning them into visual information, what theoretical framework should be invoked? From a philosophical perspective (within the history of aesthetics) the proposal can be glossed as an attempt to represent the sublime – the Kantian sublime defined as what exceeds representation (the formless). From an information theory point of view, though, the distinction made here is unreal: visualization is defined historically in terms of improvements in the representation and transmission of information. From a quantum computational point of view, data (quantitative) correspond to Kant's sublime while representation

22   In J.L. Lumley, 'Some comments on Turbulence,' *Physics of Fluids*, A, 4 (1992): 203-211.

23   Robert Ecke, 'The Turbulence problem: An Experimentalist's Perspective,' *Los Alamos Science* 29 (2005): 124-141, 124. Accessed at http://cnls.lanl.gov/External/articles/LAS_Robert_turbulence.pdf.

24   A.N. Shiryaev, 'Kolmogorov and the Turbulence,' 1-3. Accessed at http://www.maphysto.dk/publications/MPS-misc/1999/12.pdf.

as a function of quality or form corresponds to information.[25] In climate change models, where so much data is not visual (but perhaps atmospheric), Kathryn Yusoff points out, 'visualization is introduced as a tool for understanding the data – but this is a translation that happens after data capture.'[26] In this sense 'Hamlet's Mill' has to represent the impossibility of visual representation: its non-anthropomorphic form, its resistance to paraphrase, lets people contemplate the blind spot at the heart of the ambition to reduce the world to objects and images. What you see partly is that you cannot see the 'data': 'Visualizations are representations intended to convey information about data. Modelling refers to how data is (sic) collected and organized.'[27]

In the digital philosophy movement, on the other hand, nature computes; that is, the data are forms of information processing. In this case computation is an analog of natural complexity and the algorithm (or information) is, as it were, in the data. 'Natural phenomena are thus the products of computation processes. In a computational universe new and unpredictable phenomena emerge as a result of simple algorithms operating on simple computing elements such as, e.g., cellular automata, and complexity originates from the bottom-up driven emergent processes. Cellular automata are equivalent to a universal Turing machine.'[28] On this argument visualization is an unnecessary hypothesis. However, it remains essential to the communication of information to non-specialist audiences. But in this case what is visualized beyond a coincidence of metaphysical and physical frames of reference? Suppose that turbulence could be represented, what would we see? What would the visualization mean? How can a digitally configured nature flow? By the introduction of

25   Kathryn Yusoff and Brett Stalbaum, 'Leonardo Electronic Almanac Discussion (LEAD),'
      Wild Nature and Digital Life Chat, 3 January 2007. Accessed at http://www.leoalmanac.org/
      resources/lead/digiwild/bstalbaumkyusoff.asp.
26   Ibid.
27   Ibid.
28   Gordana Dodig Crnkovic, 'Dynamics of Information as Natural Computation,' *Information* 2, 3
      (2011): 460-477. Accessed at http://www.mdpi.com/2078-2489/2/3/460/htm.

randomness? Is turbulence in the architecture of natural systems? Is it different from complexity? Does it signify the evidence of non-linear patterns or their breakdown? Is there a third kind of matter to consider? Kant's sublime is formless: data are formless (or are they?). The matter of turbulence is characterized by its resemblance to colloid materials; it exhibits the qualities of glue, mucus, viscosity; it oozes or is muddy. Serres' philosophy of 'mixed bodies' applies to it; equally Latour's notion of 'hybrid objects.'[29] In other words the unit of turbulence may never be reducible to an algorithm, even one that factored in randomness. It begins as a statistically significant field. Its classic formulation is in the vortex of atoms imagined by Democritus (which exists in a Brownian medium or state). In its descent via Leonardo and Descartes, it is an instance of 'minor design'; like the interpersonal, it begins as a pirouette where two bodies simultaneously revolve around each other. For what is drawn? Lines of force and in particular vortices...

These were questions shared with research colleagues in the first days of the Sydney residency. They clarified the problem of translating between disciplines. There was, in addition, the question of evaluation. Complexity and associated turbulent behaviors appeal aesthetically to the artist but an engineer is likely to take a different view. Notwithstanding Viktor Schauberger's demonstration of the vortical organization of flowing water,[30] engineers regard turbulence as a source of chaos: vortex-induced vibrations threaten the stability of structures. The marketing of Vortex Hydro Energy may mark a reversal of this tradition but in general the idea is to neutralize flutter, tremor, etc. Choreographers encourage dancers to copy one another, introducing new, unexpected movement complexes into the collective movement form. Such explorations are of little use to a turbine designer whose object is to turn turbulence into a linear flow that generates regular energy. Atmospheric turbulence, which causes

29   Carter, *Dark Writing*, 177-187.
30   See Victor Schauberger, *The Water Wizard: The Extraordinary Properties of Natural Water*, trans. C. Coats (Oxford: Gateway Publishing, 1998).

most weather-related aircraft accidents, is set to increase because of climate change – whatever the cause of this no-one desires it; if it takes the apocalyptic scenarios presented in *An Inconvenient Truth* to bring people to their senses, who is going to quibble about compromising 'the political economy of the sublime'?[31] In other words, if climate change and turbulence are synonymous, what is the point of worrying about the details of presentation: whatever its aesthetic appeal, turbulence must be suborned to ethical considerations. We can enjoy images of complexity but not at the expense of clarifying options for future collective well-being.

To visualize complexity in the (non-) form of turbulence begged the question of value. Initial discussions between designers, artists, economists and mathematicians at UTS raised the spectre of epistemological chaos. Anti-methodical, or intuitionist moves may be tolerated within the theoretical culture of a discipline or field, but they risk a crisis in verifiability when exported across disciplinary borders. Behind this nervousness is the larger shadow cast by the normative definition of research communities, which makes the conduct of research a microcosm of the good conduct of an ordered and accountable society. Social scientists describe how a controlled flow of people can break down under the pressure of crowding: a stop-and-go pattern interrupts the laminar passage of feet and 'crowd turbulence' erupts.[32] Probably something similar is feared in the research sector: the interruption caused by an over-exposure to incommensurable perspectives can produce a turbulence manifested as a loss of self-organizational skills. When narratives lose credibility, authority breaks down. Anything can happen.

What is true internally is also true externally: doubts different disciplines may have about the implications of trying to describe complexity are amplified in the arena of educational branding, research

---

31 To quote Yusoff.
32 See, for example, Dirk Helbing, Anders Johansson and Habib Z. Al-Abideen, 'Crowd Turbulence: The Physics of Crowd Disasters,' *The Fifth International Conference on Nonlinear Mechanics*, Shanghai (2007): 967-969.

program design and resourcing and what Lyotard refers to as the challenge of knowledge 'legitimation.' Complexity is not only a feature of natural systems. It applies to the brain, to the phenomenon of consciousness; it applies to societies whose histories also demonstrate complex feedback mechanisms (culture) as well as emergent behavior (history). Complexity also applies to the organization of knowledge (witness the phenomenon of Wikipedia). In all of these situations, it is recognized that complexity tends to produce ever more complex orders, patterns, cultures or states. Order and complexity go together, spiralling round each other. However, the identification of knowledge with problem-solving militates against the recognition of this: 'In problem-solving strategies, the decision-making tree leads us to expect and select regular, deterministic, indication-dependent, functional, and linear processes, but in complex systems many processes are irregular, indeterminate, and independent from their indications, and almost all of them not-linear.'[33] It is demonstrable that our research cultures, too, are hostile to the notion of complexity as an end point of the investigative process. Their object is invariably to find a tool of reduction, regulation and prediction; it is not, for example, to produce a genuine analogue (only a consistent model). That is, it can be argued that the politics of the knowledge universities promote dictates that complexity will be anathematized either as obfuscation, deficient methodology, or as uncompetitive (in the race to produce axioms).

In short, unpredictability is a value as well as a phenomenon. At the heart of its characterization is the attitude towards creativity. Turbulence or non-linear change may be accepted as a physical fact of life, but it is only in particular circumstances (in complexity studies) that it is (partially) mathematicized as an irreducible feature of a system. More colloquially, turbulence is nature in a pre-theorized state: if things happen without apparent cause, they invite investigation, regulation – the inductive extraction of general laws from particular observations, the progressive

---

33   Rupert Riedl, 'Systems Theory of Evolution,' *Evolution and Cognition* 9, 1 (2003): 31-42, 31.

elimination of uncertainty. As the mathematicization of the universe will not be finished soon, the human implications of this theoretical approach remain obscured. Simplification passes through complexity. In the other direction the universe is produced: its reason resides in the imagination. This constructivist theory of knowledge locates creativity at the heart of sense-making. In the academy the two modes of knowledge-seeking, the reductionist and the projectivist, map respectively to the sciences and the arts; but it seemed in these early days at UTS that the digitally-mediated art of design occupied a strategically in-between position. The iterations of the design process are willfully turbulent, but the complexity of the outcomes supposes the knowability of the system.

Shadowing these exchanges was the status of design research and method as sustainable approaches to problem-solving in a cross-disciplinary context. Identifying research with process, and both with invention, could design, like the other creative arts, produce a knowledge that, as Serres puts it, expands 'Irregularly, from the local to the global'; a knowledge that 'pulsates, dances, trembles, vibrates, scintillates like a curtain of flames'[34]; that establishes a ground that will 'found local inventions to come'?[35] As Serres' language implies, such a flamboyant method is likely to found truth in the study of turbulent situations. And the forms of its knowledge are likely to retain a trace of these turbulent inspirations. In *Dark Writing*, discussing the achievement of Jesse Hartley, the chief engineer responsible for the construction of large parts of the Liverpool Docks, I transposed these concerns to the practice of place making. How could Hartley 'confidently raise five storey warehouses close to the edges of masonry walls sunk directly into the alluvial silt of the Mersey (or fragilely resting on scanty submarine rafts of wood)?... Smith and Weir (respectively experts in the history of design and in engineering conservation)... conclude that Hartley was not a civil or structural engineer, proceeding on

34   Michel Serres, *The Troubadour of Knowledge*, trans. S.F. Glaser and W. Paulson (Ann Arbor: University of Michigan Press, 1997), 165.

35   In Paul Carter, *Material Thinking*, 8.

21

the basis of mathematical calculation and physical theory, but a craftsman, whose practices were guided by successful precedent, by a feel for his materials and by the practical exigencies of the situation.'[36]

Hartley's intuitive technique was problem-based. It responded successfully to forming situations. In an illuminating discussion of the ontology of mathematics in the work of Alain Badiou and Gilles Deleuze, Daniel Smith explains how Greek geometry distinguished between theorems and problems. Theorems 'concerned the demonstration, from axioms or postulates, of the inherent properties belonging to a figure, whereas problems concerned the construction of figures using a straight edge and compass.'[37] Because of this, 'in theorematics, a deduction moves from axioms to the theorems that are derived from it, whereas in problematics a deduction moves from the problem to the ideal accidents and *events* that condition the cases that resolve it.'[38] Practice-based research of this kind belongs to what Deleuze calls 'ambulatory' science: These sciences – they include metallurgy, surveying, stonecutting and perspective – 'subordinate all their operations to the sensible conditions of intuition and construction – following the flow of matter, drawing and linking smooth space.'[39] An ominous consequence of this research style – at least from the point of view of a new arts/sciences dialogue – is that this sensitivity to fluctuations 'coextensive with reality itself' 'means that they can never be 'autonomous' – a vulnerability of which axiomatically-based science takes full advantage, at the same time making the work of the craftsman 'difficult to classify, [its] history... difficult to follow.'[40]

If design merely muddles through, its practices may bear the imprint of complex considerations, but will not produce a reliable knowledge of

---

36 Carter, *Dark Writing*, 229-230.
37 David W. Smith, 'Badiou and Deleuze on the Ontology of Mathematics,' in *Think Again: Alain Badiou and the Future of Philosophy*, ed. Peter Hallward (London: Continuum, 2004), 77-93, 79.
38 Ibid., 79-80.
39 Ibid., 84.
40 Ibid.

complexity. Designers will not be equipped to conceptualize problems outside their immediate area of craft skill and intuition. In this case, in any investigation of complexity and its visualization, design will be relegated to the representationalist role of materializing generalizations (axioms) generated independently. 'Hamlet's Mill' will be the qualitative expression of quantitative data but will hardly follow the flow of matter in its form and program. It sounds on this basis as if practice-based design research, as it is called in the Australian universities, is bound to fail, at least in the assumption of a leadership, or brokerage, role in any cross-disciplinary program of the kind outlined here. However, this conclusion rests on the assumption that design method is, simply, 'difficult to classify,' and this may not be the case. On the contrary, the iterative method of design research, the technique of continuous revision, adjustment and modification may have the energetic character of turbulence inscribed into it.

Design process is essentially a feedback loop in which production and reflection circle each other: in research, drawing and drawing out are coterminous. Hartley's gift for improvising and innovating 'depended on the impression he communicated that he was *not* inventing anything new.'[41] Likewise with design: it carries conviction when it seems to have emerged inevitably and unconsciously from 'the flow of matter.' Further, this 'flow' is tackled, encountered or intuited, not in its laminar mode, when it is inaccessible to work or manipulation, but when, as is illustrated in Leonardo da Vinci's famous drawing of an old man in profile together with water studies, it grows turbulent, forming vortices, whose strange and complex energy forms it is natural to ponder.[42] As a science of 'events,' design does not deal in linear flows but in vortical patterns. In other

---

41 Carter, *Dark Writing*, 230.
42 Leonardo da Vinci's drawing, 'An old man in profile to right, seated on a rocky ledge; water studies and a note,' c.1513, is widely reproduced. It is catalogued in *The Drawings and Miscellaneous Papers of Leonardo deVinci... atWindsor Castle*, ed. C. Pedretti, London and NewYork, 1981, p.48.

words, there is a correspondence between the field of study and the methods brought to it. Turbulence is not simply a 'complex and unpredictable cultural or physical environment.' It is the phenomenon of feedback: or, more exactly, it is the self-conscious awareness of the power of feedback mechanisms to inaugurate new behaviors. It is associated with changes of state that appear spontaneous (or unscripted) because they respond to or interact with surface phenomena in real time. As the response involves recognition or coding, the emerging states are not meaningless but incorporate, consolidate and complexify. The key is that the chameleon behaviors, guises and disguises rapidly assumed are adopted agilely, strategically – for a purpose (political, social, cultural, constructive).

In 'Whither Science? - A Science without Origins: Nomad, Minor Science and the Scientific Method,' Paulo and Alexandra Correa discuss Deleuze and Guattari's distinction between Royal Science and 'a kind of science, or treatment of science, that seems very difficult to classify... .' With reference to their account of Serres, they characterize this model of thought as 'smooth, based on continua, one that does not striate either horizontally or vertically. Its object is not static – nor is it beings or their apparent or illusory constancy – but the constant transformation or alteration of beings, their becomings, transitions and heterogeneities, the dynamic of processes.'[43] This physics of 'motion and the living', this 'eccentric or minor science' has its origins in the thought of Heraclitus. It is developed by Democritus ('atomism and vortical, curvilinear motion') and by Anaxagoras ('theory of chaos and ordered turbulence, or *nous*').[44] According to Correa and Correa, Serres and Deleuze and Guattari 'suggest that this eccentric science has an hydraulic model – the model of Archimedean science: fluids are no longer treated as solids, flow is seen as being turbulent, vortical, neither parallel nor laminar; the shortest path

---

43   Paulo N. Correa and Alexandra N. Correa, 'Whither Science? A Science Without Origins:
      Nomad, Minor Science and the Scientific Method (2),' *Journal of Science and the Politics of Thought*
      2, 1, (2009): 1-49, 2.

44   Ibid., 3

between two points can be geometrically treated as a straight line but defines the length of curve; principles of buoyancy counteract the weight of the body, etc. Eccentric science could be defined by the proposition "from turba to turbo" – from the bands or packets of atoms or inert matter, to the vortices they populate while being ordered into jets.'[45]

When design becomes a form of dark writing, it corresponds to this hydraulic model: drawing proceeds self-consciously. Drawing out of itself what is new, it exists in a continuously self-modifying dialogue with its origin. Brodsky-Lacour makes a brilliant point when she argues that the distinction of the 'one dimensional' Cartesian line was its idealism, the fact that it was drawn out of itself without apparent reference to the external world – 'Descartes' "well-ordered [modern] towns and public squares that an engineer traces on a vacant plan according to his free imaginings [or, fancy]" not only depended on erasing the traces of earlier, "poorly proportioned" cities, they depended on drawing as such'[46] – but her argument may be overdrawn. For his 'architectonic line' may still have aimed to express the architecture of matter. Hence Correa & Correa classify 'Descartes' minor theory of Aether vortices, aiming to explain gravitational action without recourse to action-at-a-distance [as] another salient example of eccentric science, one that attempts to apply Archimedean principles of buoyancy to the motions of cosmic bodies.'[47] From an ethical point of view, what matters is not the motion/non-motion antithesis – the logical line versus the mimetic one – but the 'which motion?': 'Striated motion along straight lines, light rays or rehabilitated geodesics, motion that counts Space in order to occupy it – or vortical motion, wave motion, motion with intrinsic measures, that occupies Space as it generates it, in the strictest of senses.'[48]

45 Ibid.
46 Carter, *Dark Writing*, 195.
47 Correa and Correa, 'Whither Science?', 15.
48 Ibid., 37.

3. Design as Dramaturgy

Transposed into the realm of public space design, Correa & Correa's 'minor science of becoming' dissolves the figure/ground distinction, which, in planning discourse, defines (or confines) the real world application of design. Instead of measuring space, quantifying and fixing intervals, proportions and relations, a turbulent practice produces its own space, one that, while remaining topologically consistent, is elastic, variable and alterable. The design is wherever the designer and his/her 'forming situation' are; and everyone, or at least the 'public,' is involved in its vortical enfolding and unfolding. The public space designer of this type can be compared to the new breed of dramaturg who, in certain kinds of post-dramatic performance, replaces the traditional director.[49] In his influential paper, 'The Deep Order Called Turbulence: The Three Faces of Dramaturgy,' Eugenio Barba described a 'dramaturgy of changing states' charged with anxiety and ambivalence, as inherently ambiguous instinctual physical movement wrestles with the conventionally delimiting constraints of symbolic language, generating what Barba effectively calls 'turbulence.'[50] Unpredictability is written into the new script but what emerges makes a new kind of sense, for turbulence is vortical: 'It engenders vortexes that upset the current of narrative action. In the absence of these vortexes the continuity, rhythm, and narrative risk lapsing into the obvious, into mere illustration.'[51]

Contributors to 'On Turbulence,' a recent issue of *Performance Research*, amplify and apply these remarks in a wide range of different contexts and practices.[52] Most of the turbulent situations they evoke could, however, be

---

49   With reference to new theatre practices described by Hans-Thies Lehmann in *Postdramatic Theatre*, trans. Karen Jürs-Munby (London: Routledge, 1999).

50   Eugenio Barba, 'The Deep Order Called Turbulence: the Three Faces of Dramaturgy,' trans. J. Barba, *The Drama Review* 44, 4 (2000): 56-66.

51   Ibid., 61.

52   Paul Carter, ed., 'On Turbulence,' *Performance Research*, 16, 5 (2014).

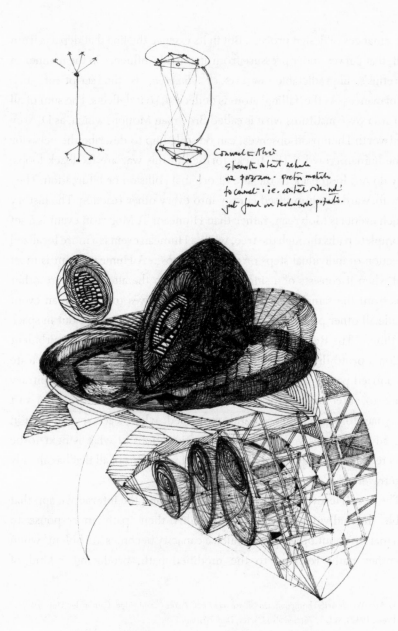

Involute 4, artline texta 0.4 on paper, 210 x 297 mm, February 2012. A45, 27.

performances of design process. But in its essence the line that departs from itself, that curves under pressure from an outside influence in the manner of Lucretius's unpredictable swerve or *clinamen*, is the script of such performances. As the 'falling' atom is deflected, so it deflects. The sum of all such swerves constitutes what is called Brownian Motion, which, as D'Arcy Wentworth Thompson observes, can be scaled up to describe the behavior of the human crowd.[53] The tracks formed in this way are feedback loops. They do not loop back to the site of original collision or bifurcation. They carry forward this impressed energy into every other reaction. The history of such events is Moivrean, rather than Humean: 'A Moivrean event is a set of complete paths through the tree, while a Humean event is a more localized collection of individual steps or chains of steps... A Humean event is most local when it consists of a single step, and then the alternatives are other steps from the same starting point. The alternatives to a Moivrean event include all other paths through the tree, and these may spread out in space and time.'[54] The Romantic writer, Thomas de Quincey, gives this turbulent motion a proto-dramaturgical character when he reflects, 'Every intricate and untried path in life, where it was from the first a matter of arbitrary choice to enter upon it or avoid it, is effectually a path through a vast Hercynian forest, unexplored and unmapped, where each several turn in your advance leaves you open to new anticipations of what is next to be expected, and consequently open to altered valuations of all that has already been traversed.'[55]

The new 'Hercynian forest' is the internet and the interactive app that enable the individual navigator to modify their 'path' in response to information about other 'paths.' Such a capacity becomes 'turbulent' when the other paths respond to the modified path, producing a kind of

---

53   D'Arcy Wentworth Thompson, *On Growth and Form*, 2 vols (Cambridge: Cambridge University Press, 1942), vol. 1, 76. See also Carter, *Dark Writing*, 179.

54   Glenn Shafer, *The Art of Causal Conjecture* (Cambridge, Mass.: The MIT Press, 1996), 24.

55   David Masson, ed., *The Collected Writings of Thomas De Quincey* (London: A. & C. Black, 1896-1897), vol. III, 314-315.

maelstrom of mutually altering and converging paths. In performance, a turbulent state obtains when the phenomenon of mutual modification becomes the basis of the work. A place-based app can show many people where they are in the city in relation to various phenomena; accordingly, it influences their navigation of the city.[56] However, it only becomes a turbulent event when the individuals using the service start to modify their behavior in relation to one another, whereupon a collectivity begins to emerge, self-organizing and unpredictable. The iSkyTV project of the Institute for Infinitely Small Things, for example, seems to work across these levels of self-awareness/self-organization. Comparable self-aware feedback loops occur in the transitional zone between ritual and historical re-enactment – and between both these layers of twice remembered behavior and the situation where the participants are collectively responsible for devising the new work. This observation applies to certain kinds of performance,[57] but also to the dynamics of cross-cultural encounter. In such cases of mimetic self-modification, a potential exists to improvise new rules of sociability.[58]

Such interactions are obviously creative but their power to invent new rules of coexistence adequate to the complexity of the situation depends on the willingness of the participants to reflect on their habitual behavior. In pedagogy this self-reflexive and self-organizing potential corresponds to Gregory Bateson's idea of learning about learning or deutero-learning.[59] Chris Argyris discusses 'double loop learning'[60] and, in another spatio-choreographical metaphor, the psychologist Kurt Lewin speaks about a

---

56   See, for example, Esmeralda Kosmatopoulos's 'Mark It' project.

57   The Indigenous music theatre work Trepang is a good case in point. See Peta Stephenson, *The Outsiders Within: Telling Australia's Indigenous-Asian Story* (Sydney: University of New South Wales Press, 2007), 51-57.

58   See Carter, *Meeting Place*, 56.

59   See Max Wisser, 'Gregory Bateson on Deutero-Learning and Double Bind: A Brief Conceptual History,' *Journal of History of the Behavioral Sciences* 39, 3 (2000): 269-278. Published online in Wiley InterScience (www.interscience.wiley.com). DOI: 10.1002/

60   Chris Argyris, 'Double-Loop Learning, Teaching and Research,' *Academy of Management Learning & Education* 1, 2 (2002): 206-219.

theory and practice of social action involving a 'spiral of steps.'[61] When feedback leading to turbulence, or complex cascades of events that cannot be prescribed, occurs, the 'director' yields to the 'dramaturg': instead of actors passively following directions, the new organizer is like Leonardo's old man pondering the whirlpool, experimentally lowering a staff into its chaos to observe the effect.

In the field of design, the appeal of the new dramaturgy may find expression in the slipperiness of the terms 'architect' and 'designer.' The designer may be the architect as dramaturg. The impact of this reformulation may be felt in the work practices of the studio, in a new collective ownership of, and participation in, the iterative design process. But its obvious expression is in the interface between the designer and the tools of parametric modeling. In this context Telmao Santos argues that the incorporation of digital technology into the 'plot' of performance disturbs the traditional 'co-presencing' said to differentiate performance: it mediates cascades of reflexive transformations that put into question the constitution of the self, the nature of the collectivity and the possibility of stable representations. To bring turbulence into performance practice is, he contends, to renounce any idea of working from analogy: instead, a comparable scaffolding of initial conditions tending to produce multiplying modifications and transformations has to be built. To be in the flow one has to start in the flow.[62]

The comparison with the forming situation which precipitates the designer's work is complete. In essence CAD establishes 'initial conditions' that have no analogy in the real world; but through a process of mimetic modification they bend towards real world representations. In the other direction, the space they produce is topologically self-consistent. Its points of reference are internally consistent, reactive and interactive but

61   Kurt Lewin, *Resolving Social Conflicts: Selected Papers on Group Dynamics* (New York: Harper & Row, 1947), 206.

62   Telma João Santos, 'On Turbulence: In Between Mathematics and Performance,' *Performance Research* 16, 5 (2014): 7-12.

do not necessarily correspond to any object in the external world that can be represented. This does not mean, though, that the plans, sections and perspectives produced in CAD represent nothing. Parametric design tools, for instance, may visualize De Quincey's immensely complex 'intricate and untried path,' the sensation anyone moving through an environment has that all the points shift in relation to one's passage. The sense of being enveloped by a space that warps, contracts, billows out and enfolds in relation to oneself has been variously described in terms of 'reversed' or 'curvilinear' perspective, and the corollary of perceiving oneself inside an elastically modifiable net is the alteration of one's own movement. The archetypal practitioner of this psycho-spatial feedback looping is the hunter, who has the sensation that the tracker and what is tracked are glued together down a constantly self-departing path or arc.

The environment navigated in this way is a 'second skin,' an eido-kinetically responsive flowing garment or fluid medium.[63] In this context, it seems slightly perverse, at least in retrospect, that the well-known Second Skin workshops started at the Architectural Association in 2001, should have invoked the sense of touch when their technique for inducing 'a seamless interface between the individual's mind and surroundings' was so relentlessly mentalist: using hypnosis to extract 'deeply rooted conception or schemas that are closely tied to the emotional states and the body's extended intelligence through the central nervous system,' their aim was to translate these patterns or schemata into objects (such as a 'house') that were 'a reflection of the person.'[64] A far more persuasive 'new emergent approach to architecture' that contested 'predetermined codes, textbook, fashion and architects' dictatorial spaces' would be one that originated in the feedback across the surface between the 'micro' and the 'macro.' Hence, another contributor to 'On Turbulence,' Kanta Kochhar-

---

63   On the eidokinetic intuition, see Carter *Dark Writing*, 267-271.

64   Marcos Lutyens, 'Second Skin, St. Paul's Gallery, Fierce Festival, Birmingham, UK,' accessed at http://www.mlutyens.com/second-skin,-st.-pauls-gallery,-fierce-festival,-birmingham,-uk,-2003.html#.VPvCrjlqv8t

Lindgren, in an article subtitled 'Touching Cities, Visual Tactility, and Windows,' meets the same objectives as the Second Skin group – the identification of the person with their dwelling space – through 'a type of mobile architectonics, an art of constructing systems, in which we come to know not who we are, but *where we are* through making ourselves in the interstitial spaces of the city, through the galvanic responses that pass from city to body and from body to city, and across the multitude of bodies in action all around us.'[65] In Kochhar-Lindgren's practice touching produces a new city formed of second-order reflections, pressure points and weights. The new 'line' is not linear (smooth) but a 'mutable edge.' These are the resources and techniques of parametric drawing transposed to the realm of proprioceptive touch and retooled as a technique of urban pattern recognition. Kochhar-Lindgren characterizes her work as artistic research into the potential of 'revelatory turbulence' to transform social relations.

4. 'Hamlet's Mill'

The greatest obstacle to the visualization of complexity may be visualism, an impoverished sense of sight as the registration and valorization of fixed objects stably related in empty space. It is a visualism that cannot visualize the feedback between parts that may be one of the primary means of repressing turbulence. Once one acknowledges the turbulent constitution of nature, meteorology, biology – and, indeed, the endlessly complex feedback processes that maintain equilibrium in any system (economic, moral, social) – it becomes astonishing that no evidence of these surfaces in our dominant cultures of representation. Such notions as the sovereign subject, linear logic and even the cult of smoothness in design seem like

---

65   Kanta Kochhar-Lindgren, 'The Turbulence project: Touching Cities, Visual Tactility, and Windows,' *Performance Research* 16, 5 (2014): 13-21, 14.

Involute 5, artline texta 0.4 on paper, 210 x 297 mm, June 2006. A38, 21.

forms of psychological infantilism: as if the psyche could not confront the turbulence of living in the midst of it all. The gaze with its valorization of fixity, focus, outline and image suddenly appears autistic. In contrast, the other sense of the world, touch, may acquire a new heuristic value: in touching it is impossible to say whether we touch or are touched; in self touching we experience a discharge across the skin that is indistinguishable from the phenomenon of feedback in other contexts.

Touch, which can be extended to other modes of proprioceptive engagement with the world such as hearing and, indeed, physical movement, not only re-narrates the architectural void as a second skin palpable everywhere. It introduces a different temporality. Things are not fixed (visually) in their place and sequence; they aggregate at the surfaces where two bodies meet. In choreographing moments of touch (sought and unsought) a different history of space emerges, vortical, occasional and turbulent. To brush up against the unknown can be, if properly dramaturged, a therapeutic process, as Pil Hansen (another 'On Turbulence' contributor) narrates. Touching is not simply a different tool of worldly navigation or a form of intimate communication: it describes an emotion induced at a distance. To be touched is to be infected with some else's mania, suffering or humanity. It is, fundamentally, to be stirred up, agitated. If it leads to a tumult of tears, it would not be surprising or out of place. In other words, as Hansen's account of Karen Kaeja's project illustrates, touch is a collective projection, pivoted between attraction and repulsion. Reconceived as a dynamic force, drawing out and drawing in, its power to shape the future as well as repair past wounds emerges. In short, to be touched is also to identify emotionally with something observed. It is a different way of seeing the world. The empathetic, mutually modifying and self-transforming behavioural feedback loops that characterize a 'revelatory turbulence' would be impossible without this multisensory mode of seeing.[66]

---

66   Pil Hansen with Karen Kaeja and Ame Henderson, 'Transference and Transition in Systems of Dance Generation,' *Performance Research* 16, 5 (2014): 23-33.

Proprioceptive modes of environmental apprehension not only define the self-organizing performances of the new dramaturgy. They conform to the new epistemology proposed by Correa & Correa, who, in promoting their 'Aether theory' as a way of overcoming scientific dualism, discuss 'the ethics of knowledge and the aesthetics of art and science.' They suggest that in 'the dualist mindset what is felt (*senti*) is already what is resented ("re-senti") by it, the trace of the sensation or of the feeling, the prolongation of an emotion but caught in a system of reaction that inverts the perceived and estranges the "felt". A veil descends upon feeling, perceiving and thinking.'[67] They see this estrangement leading to the impoverishment of science and its retreat into relativism. Instead of striving to understand the nature of reality, scientists limit themselves to 'filling a particular axiom with measurements, observations and experiments that only "make sense" if that axiom is assumed.'[68] This is in line with the Deleuzian distinction between Royal and ambulatory sciences or, in Smith's terms, the axiomatic and the theorematic.

Interestingly for us, they cite 'the fad of global warming (now called "climate change")' as an example of impoverished, or desensitized scientific method, commenting, 'only when desire will become able to form adequate ("clear and concise") ideas of its object, will it become rational, come to find reason as a sense amongst others; and for that it needs an active joy, an emotion that shirks sentiment and human sentimentality, an emotion that creates... and a method that connects, that makes adequate connections, connections that function – the real functionalist method of science.'[69]

Where, one wonders, does this leave 'Hamlet's Mill' and the proposal to create a public monitor of complex change? Can a 'clear and precise' idea of turbulence be formed? And, if so, by what method?

In early iterations of the project we rehearsed the history of scientific visualization, and employing Kantian schemata of our own, tried to

---

67   Correa and Correa, 'Whither Science?,' 37.
68   Ibid., 39.
69   Ibid.

articulate the challenge of the new arts/science research program in terms of a revivified sublime. The turbulence of change defines a boundary to what can be represented. If, as Kant argued, the order and regularity of nature is introduced by the intellect, then the disorder and irregularity of the maelstrom transcends reason (and its representations). This is not to say that the turbulence of change is wholly removed from the realm of perception. It is just that it cannot be looked at in a way that will furnish an image of it. It is like looking into the vortex of the whirlpool, which is both something and nothing, a kind of eye that swallows up vision. Such is the 'saturated phenomenon' which 'refuses to let itself be regarded as an [abject] object... precisely because it appears with a multiple and indescribable excess that annuls all effort at constitution [assimilation to an abstract concept].'[70] Confronted with the exceptional, the gaze can no longer discern the 'poor or common phenomenality of objects... hence, there arrives "counter-experience of a non-object".'[71]

It is in reason's blind spot, described here, that the sublime emerges; for the sublime involves a kind of blinding, one that 'Hamlet's Mill' models with its endlessly changing field of scintillations: 'For intuition, supposedly "blind" in the realm of poor or common phenomena, turns out, in a radical phenomenology, to be blinding.'[72] 'Bedazzlement begins when perception crosses its tolerable maximum... .'[73] The artwork is located where the gaze of the world (in our case the void at the heart of the maelstrom) intersects the human gaze. It is the moment (the *Augenblick*) in which the eye (*Auge*) and the gaze (*Blick*) briefly meet and pass through each other. This, at least, was how we were theorizing the challenge in 2007: to design a work, or perhaps a performance, or even a region in public space where the unrepresentable and the representable

70   Jean-Luc Marion, *Being Given: Toward a Phenomenology of Givenness*, trans. J.L. Kosky (Stanford CA: Stanford University Press, 2002), 213.

71   Ibid., 215.

72   Ibid., 203.

73   Ibid., 206.

intersected, a zone where, in the glare of the sublime, the perceptual field acquired a second skin. As noted, in climate change models, where so much data is 'not visual (but perhaps atmospheric),' Kathryn Yusoff points out, 'visualization is introduced as a tool for understanding the data – but this is a translation that happens after data capture.'[74] 'Hamlet's Mill' represented the impossibility of visual representation: its non-anthropomorphic form, its resistance to paraphrase, let people contemplate the blind spot at the heart of the ambition to reduce the world to objects and images. Its public education program would partly be to see through seeing, to reintegrate seeing and sensing, to encourage a visualization free of *resentment*.

These thought paths through the 'Hercynian forest' of conceptualizing and communicating complex change implied 'several turns' towards the challenge presented by the digital philosophy movement and their contention that data are forms of information processing. Even if the algorithm (or information) is an analog of natural complexity, it has to be discovered and the framework of complexity (the field of data and their definition) has to be constructed. The conclusion digital philosophers reach is susceptible to the principle of infinite logical regression. As pattern recognition is essential to their argument, the tools used to detect physical phenomena and the equations developed to explain them (whether the explanations are correspondences or constructions) remain modeling devices. It is true that there is an economy and rigour about their position, based on the conviction that the cosmos is mathematics all the way down, but their position is obviously vulnerable to Correa and Correa's critique of axiomatically pursued science. In this austere context 'Hamlet's Mill' is, if nothing else, an ethical response to the challenge of communicating complexity. Whether or not it is adequately grounded – as an instance of ambulatory arts/science collaboration it was always 'vulnerable' to stronger, more generalized descriptions of the phenomena

---

74   Yusoff and Stalbaum, 'Leonardo Electronic Almanac Discussion (LEAD).'

– it seeks to arouse that 'desire' in us that will enable us to 'to form adequate ("clear and concise") ideas of its object.'

After all, descending from the lofty heights of computational theory, 'Hamlet's Mill' was originally conceived in relation to a forming situation where the question of computational models and their impact on public opinion was in question. In one early 'turn' of the 'several paths' of the project, 'Hamlet's Mill' was an invitation to respond to a community awareness program recommended in the report 'Thames Estuary 2100, Managing Flood Risk through London and the Thames estuary.' 'Hamlet's Mill' was, in this dialogue, presented as a strategy for reconciling an obvious paradox of the climate change discourse – that in other arenas of democratic-capitalistic endeavour change was welcomed. It seemed inconsistent to expect our most creative thinkers to argue against change in this one domain. The thinking behind this was a measured reaction to the unexpected public resistance to well-intentioned initiatives like *An Inconvenient Truth* to galvanize political and civil action to mitigate the effects of climate change. Gore's film showed a 'hot crisis.'[75] The phenomenon of global warming is presented as a story of 'immediate and concrete risk.'[76] It manipulates an 'information deficit' model of public awareness and understanding of climate change, assuming that people are rational, responsible actors that merely need the right information in order to alter their behaviors and support policy change.[77] We say *manipulate* because in a later interview Gore admitted that the visualizations used in the film exaggerated. He defended 'an over-representation of factual presentations on how dangerous [global warming] is' on the grounds that 'Nobody is interested in solutions if they don't think there's a problem.'[78]

---

75 Emily Potter and Candice Oster, 'Communicating climate change: public responsiveness and matters of concern,' *Media International Australia* 127, 2008, 116-126, 121.
76 Ibid., 122.
77 Ibid., 118-120.
78 *The Australian*, November 26, 2009.

Efforts to remedy an 'information deficit' appear to produce a kind of imaginal flooding. It is as if the hyper-real digital images of apocalypse saturate our capacity to visualize the future differently. In an effort to produce a telling image, the climate-change Cassandras disable the imagination from acting to make sense of what is presented. Paradoxically, creativity – the power to change the way things are – is petrified. The attempt to refloat a devalued visual economy has the unfortunate effect of producing representational inflation. The victim of this is symbolic literacy. Mircea Eliade emphasizes that symbolic thinking is not an aesthetic choice. It is a way of gaining access to truths that one dimensional signs cannot communicate: 'the function of a symbol is precisely that of revealing a whole reality, inaccessible to other means of knowledge: the coincidence of opposites, for example, which is so abundantly and simply expressed by symbols, is not given anywhere in the Cosmos, nor is it accessible to man's immediate experience, nor to discursive thinking.'[79] Symbolic logic of this kind is not simply a way of revealing certain truths: it is a way of communicating. Put another way, the polysemous potential of symbolic forms (what Eliade capitalizes as 'the Images') suggests the immanence of change: already complex, symbols make the possibility of greater complexity accessible. By contrast, enhanced representations (or signs) of disaster (storms, tsunamis, desertification) merely intensify the present disaster – which is, in a way, due to what Eliade describes as 'the disfavor and failure of the "man without imagination".'[80]

In this context, the production of an 'Image' has to mean constructing an image of change. The turbulence that Leonardo managed to represent in his already mentioned drawing, 'Old man in profile to right, seated on a rocky ledge; water studies and a note,' is such an image. Leonardo's drawing has always produced a distorted after-image for me, in which the old man's staff is dipped into the flood. In this wish-fulfilment a feedback loop is illustrated

---

79   Mircea Eliade, *Images and Symbols*, trans. P. Mairet (Princeton: Princeton University Press, 1991), 177.

80   Ibid., 20.

between what Correa & Correa call a 'thing-event' and a 'sense-event.' A knowledge of nature's forces is inseparable from the old man's equipment (the divining rod-like stick), but, more significantly, cannot be divorced from his interest – his observational stance or attraction to the 'data' (or flow) in question. In reality, the job of perturbation-forming is done by the rudder-shape of the lock gate but the foundation of Leonardo's scientific knowledge in the feedback loop between what is produced and what is reproduced is uncompromised. As a dramaturg of changing states, Leonardo's method is the prototype of Deleuze's 'ambulatory' science. Whatever form it took, 'Hamlet Mill's' functionality would depend on its aesthetic appeal (the Image it communicated) being the visualization of the process that produced it.

Brett Stalbaum identifies 'Kant's sublime (a function of quantity) with data, and his notion of beauty (a function of quality or form) with information.'[81] In relation to this, Correa and Correa explain, 'The real challenge of science is its minor becoming, but in the precise sense of a search for the functions, the energy functions, which create the thing or the event - which creates the "thing-event" *and* the immanent "sense-event" of thing or an event.'[82] This goal corresponds to the production of an 'artwork' when it 'provides the intrinsic logic of the composition of that artwork – a logic that is not separable from the knowledge of the logic of sensation, and which can only be conveyed by the knowledge of and the mastery of media, materials and the elements of composition.'[83] Here, 'The sense of a sensation is a function, as is the sense of a concept; the senses of things, artwork or natural things – the senses of sensations, perceptions – and the senses of ideas are, like the senses of forces or values (axiology), their functions, their intrinsic articulations that inevitably call forth a context (the context that alone confers sense)… An idea is wrong if it cannot account for the relationships it seeks to establish, explain and

---

81   Yusoff and Stalbaum, 'Leonardo Electronic Almanac Discussion (LEAD).'

82   Correa and Correa, 'Whither Science?,' 40.

83   Ibid.

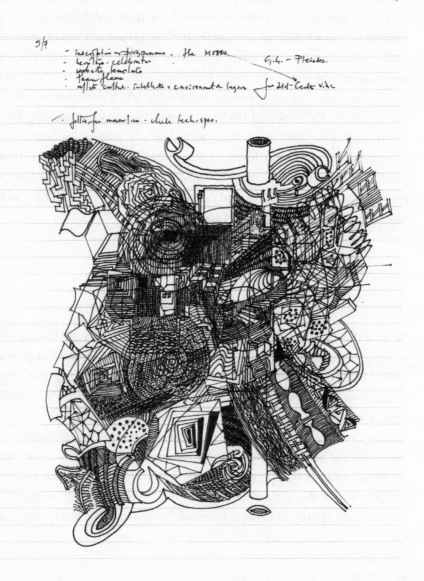

Involute 6, artline texta 0.4 on paper, 210 x 297 mm, July 2006. A38, 23.

condense; if it decontextualizes the relation. And an idea is stupid if it seeks to establish no account of relation, or denies the existence of a relation so as not to have an account for it.'[84] At this point, a 'minor science' and a 'minor art' become indistinguishable in their ethical goal. Correa and Correa take issue with Asger Jorn's prioritizing of art over science, suggesting his notion of invention, as scientific art, is common to both.[85] They criticize his notion of the empty form, the good-for-nothing free invention, saying that every innovation 'already carries its function... Ornament, the beautiful form, is not a useless form, any more than powder or saltpetre is an empty form... Ornament ornates something – it is a function of something, and it is there – ornating something – as a function of logic, an aesthetics of the beautiful.'[86]

5. Context is Everything

Despite their quibble over Jorn's privileging of art, Correa and Correa are in broad agreement with the 'aesthetic doctrine' put forward in Jorn's 1952-1963 compilation *Luck and Chance*. Jorn rails against the disinterestedness of the scientific method, but so do our authors, as their new scientific criterion – 'the senses of things' – depends on the investigator *not* being disinterested. 'The essence of aesthetics is unconditional and immediate interest or spontaneous reaction, and the aesthetic object is that phenomenon which invokes (sic) this immediate interest, whilst the aesthetic subject is the field of immediate interest.'[87] The aesthetic quality of a concept, a model, a work, a theorem or, for that

---

84   Ibid., 41.

85   Ibid., 43.

86   Ibid., 45.

87   Asger Jorn, 'Luck and Chance,' in *The Natural Order and Other Texts*, trans. P. Shield (Farnham, UK: Ashgate, 2002), 241.

matter, a natural object, is a function of our interest. However, this formulation avoids being a tautology because of the turbulent nature of interest, its attraction to 'everything unknown or enigmatic,'[88] which, in another register, could be called complexity. Curiosity or interest exists in a feedback loop with the unknown, and, according to Jorn, this is a universal condition – 'the whole biological world can be perceived as a collected interdependence,' 'a causal unity [exists] between the forms of reaction of the organic and the inorganic worlds'[89] – so that aesthetics is not a sub-branch of the study of art but an ontological stance, one that takes the unknown or 'the effects of chance'[90] as its starting point. Such a 'science of human interest attempts to gather exact knowledge about hitherto unknown phenomena';[91] it unites art and science in the pursuit of a single transcendent goal – 'aesthetics as the law of change.'[92]

By another route, then, we arrive at the threshold of a new kind of research program. Rebadged as interested science, aesthetics and the artistic production corresponding to its values, expands to fill the known (and unknown) universe. In contrast with Royal Science's stance of detached observation leading to 'numerical objectivity,'[93] Jorn's 'aesthetic perception of philosophy' focuses on the chance inherent in change. The problem is, as it were, to give this taste for turbulence any objective value. Translated into design terms, the challenge is to differentiate one design response to the visualization of complexity from another. Earlier iterations of 'Hamlet's Mill' toyed with the creation of a 'wordcoil' installed in the Turbine Hall of the Tate Modern, burrowing, Matta-Clark-like, through the roof, or an Archimedean Screw located across the bank of the Thames adjacent to Bankside's Globe Theatre. However, neither of these could

---

88   Ibid., 237.
89   Ibid., 236.
90   Ibid., 238.
91   Ibid., 240.
92   Ibid., 243.
93   Ibid., 309.

demonstrate a functional relationship with the phenomenon in question. They used the classic (and scientifically valid) form of the vortex, double spiral or volute, programming them to draw attention to the non-linear character of change, but such armatures could not, for example, meet Gregory Bateson's criterion of cybernetic explanation where, apart from '*restraints*,' 'the pathways of change would be governed only by equality of probability.'[94] In other words the successful design for the visualization of information about complex change would be one that defined the relevant 'restraints.' The essence of a feedback loop is the flexibility of its components: parts must be able to flex in relation to one another. If 'Flexibility may be defined as uncommitted potentiality for change,'[95] our approach was too pre-planned or programmatic. We were behaving like the very 'human planners and engineers' whom Bateson criticizes, whose 'products... are constructed to meet specified needs in a much more direct manner, and are correspondingly less viable';[96] that is, less 'viable' because less contextualized.

Contextualization is, for both Jorn and Bateson, the foundation of the value attached to any description, explanation or construction. Value, according to Jorn, is produced through a continuous feedback loop between community and cosmos. We cannot grasp the whole of the cosmos; instead, recognizing the 'universal subjectivity of matter,'[97] we inhabit 'local circles of value'; the function of the artist is to maintain this 'context or circle of interest for and in itself.'[98] In Correa and Correa's terms, it is this 'mutual community' that enables an idea to 'account for the relationships it seeks to establish.' Similarly, Bateson warns his readers that actions do not occur 'in' a context:

---

94   Bateson, *Steps Towards an Ecology of Mind*, 405.

95   Ibid., 505.

96   Bateson, *Steps Towards an Ecology of Mind*, 508.

97   Jorn, 'Luck and Chance,' 309.

98   Ibid.

It is important to see the particular utterance or action as part of the ecological subsystem called context and not as the product or effect of what remains of the context after the piece which we want to explain has been cut off from it. [99]

This was written at the end of the 1960s: in the period of parametric drawing, its revolutionary tenor may seem softened. Where the context or field and the operations performable by it are mutually dependent and co-existent, everything is contextual. Identity fuses into identification; space acquires regions; time becomes *involuted*, to borrow Thomas de Quincey's term; the 'emergencies' on which governments and the media trade, yield to what Brian Massumi describes as 'the supercharged proto-territory of emergence,' characterized by the 'reiterative playing out of its formative forcing' or, translated into concrete everyday terms, what one sees whenever a game of football or rugby is played, where the constant unfolding of new situations produces one emergency after another within the field of emergence, creating, as Massumi puts it, 'conditions for a plurality of extensive distinctions and their iterative regeneration.' [100]

Where does this leave design? The Platonic trend of the 'aesthetic object' – its growing identification with the totality of what it is possible to make sense of – seems to invest it with an interest in chance as such. Any modality of design predicated on place and place making – at least when they are conceived theatrically as the social engineering of a precinct – looks like the relic of a pre-cybernetic, representationalist epoch, one that has yet to heed Bateson's advice (written for a conference of planners in 1970) that a 'healthy "single system of environment combined with high human civilization" (is one) in which the flexibility of the civilization shall match that of the environment to create an ongoing complex system, open-ended for slow change of even basic (hard-programmed)

99   Bateson, *Steps Towards an Ecology of Mind*, 508.
100 Brian Massumi, 'National Enterprise Emergency: Steps Toward an Ecology of Powers': 1-22, 9.
     Accessed at www.mollecular.org/wp.../BM.National-enterprise-emergency.doc.

characteristics.'[101] Or, looking at the same challenge from the point of view of the sublime, how is a pattern to be located within the realm of chance? Pattern, to return to the digital information theorists, is nature: as Michel Serres indicates, it is information flows, communication, all the way down: 'Dolphins and bees communicate, and so do ants, and winds, and currents in the sea. Living things and inert things bounce off each other unceasingly; there would be no world without this inter-linking web of relations, a billion times interwoven.'[102] This is not Platonic but pre-Socratic, or Ionian, that is, it promotes a materialism of flux, something like the 'flowing together' that Serres evokes with his 'living syrrhesis, that combines sea and islands. In a completely new sense, the organism is synchronous for meanings and directions, for the continuous and discontinuous, for the local and the global; it combines memory, invariance, plan, message, loss, redundancy, and so forth. It is old, mortal, and the transmitter of a new cycle.'[103]

What is this organism, which, it seems, must overwhelm the 'dry land' of reason? Freud's unconscious is not inside us but everywhere or, rather, it is wherever energy has yet to be translated into information. Repression in this reformulation serves to filter 'an ocean of noise' for what can inform 'the tiny island of reality' called the 'rational.' We are language creatures and our bodies process the noise of nature for information. It is not that nature, with its storm and stress, is not always with us; rather, biologically, we are drawn to separate ourselves, to self-organise, watching the 'packages of chance... come crashing at our feet, like the surf at the edge of the beach, in the forms of eros and death. We are indeed blind to nature's 'destructive randomness' – 'Save for exceptional instances, we

101 Bateson, *Steps Towards an Ecology of Mind*, 502.

102 Michel Serres, *Angels: A Modern Myth*, trans. F. Cowper (Paris: Flammarion, 1995), 47.

103 Michel Serres, 'The Origin of Language: Biology, Information Theory, & Thermodynamics,' in Josue V. Harari and David F. Bell, eds., *Hermes: Literature, Science, Philosophy* (Baltimore: The Johns Hopkins University Press, 1982). Accessed at http://mysite.pratt.edu/~arch543p/readings/origin_of_language.html.

perceive almost nothing of this intense chaos which nonetheless exists and functions, as experiments have demonstrated conclusively. We are submerged to our neck, to our eyes, to our hair, in a furiously raging ocean. We are the voice of this hurricane, this thermal howl, and we do not even know it. It exists but it goes unperceived.'[104] The maelstrom of vortical violence is not unexpected, simply unperceived and the best that the human mind can hope for is to achieve the strange glory of the maelstrom itself, 'virtually stable turbulence within the flow.'[105]

Still, even the maelstrom has a location: in fact, the maelstrom is, like the vortex in Descartes's celestial mechanics, unthinkable except as a concrete location or region within the general noise or flux.[106] An interested science, one capable of supporting the design of the aesthetic object, would mark the interface between turbulence and flow. It would hint at something beyond itself that could not be represented but which could, nevertheless, be sensed. To a large extent, the meaning of the work would reside in the noise that surrounded and threatened to engulf it:

> The engineers believe that they can avoid the complexities and diffi-
> culties introduced into communication theory by the concept of
> 'meaning'... however... the concept 'Redundancy' is at least a partial
> synonym of 'meaning'... if the receiver can guess at missing parts of
> the message, then those parts which are received must, in fact, carry a
> meaning which refers to the missing parts and is information about
> those parts.[107]

Bateson's speculation finds experimental support in the field of hearing where, according to Albert Bregman, the enemy of auditory perception is

---

104 Ibid.
105 Ibid.
106 Hence the maelstrom is also 'The Maelstrom,' a physical feature off the Norwegian coast.
107 Albert Bregman, *Auditory Scene Analysis: The Perceptual Organization of Sound*, (Cambridge, Mass.: MIT Press, 1990), 376.

not so much noise as silence. In studies of how experimental subjects make sense of what they hear, much attention has been paid to what is known as the continuity illusion. This occurs where 'the experimenter deletes parts of a softer signal and replaces them with a louder sound, and the listener hears the softer sound as continuing unbroken behind the louder one.'[108] Taking this a step further, experimenters have compared the effect of deleting parts of the signal and replacing them with silences. Thus Miller and Licklider compared speech that was interrupted by periodic gaps (about ten times per second) to speech in which these gaps were filled by louder white noise. Repeating these and similar experiments more recent researchers have found that filling the gaps by noise can actually improve the accuracy of recognition, and hence phoneme restoration.[109]

Why should this be? Bregman speculates that the noise eliminates false transitions from sound to silence and vice versa that are interfering with the recognition of the sounds. In addition, because silences are interpreted as part of the speech itself and not as an added sound, the rhythmic introduction of silences is heard as a rhythm of the speech itself and disrupts the listener's perception of any natural rhythms that may have been in the original speech.'[110] This is a critical point in the evolution of a theory of complexity design, as what applies to audition may also apply to visualization. In both a *pars pro toto* principle operates. Messages are perceived as part of 'a larger universe within which that message creates redundancy or predictability.'[111] It is not necessary to represent everything: what is left out also communicates. Communication, whether it is digital, analogic, iconic or metaphoric, is synecdochic (a part is named in place of the whole).[112] Comprehension in this environment does not occur against a dead background (or silence) but depends on being in the flow. The

---

108 Ibid., 376.
109 Ibid.
110 Ibid.
111 Bateson, *Steps Towards an Ecology of Mind*, 421.
112 Ibid.

movement or momentum of the communicating gesture overflows beyond its strict signification to hint at patterns swirling out before and after. In speech, intonation – which the poet Marina Tsvetayeva defines as 'an intention, which has become a sound'[113] – represents this phenomenon. In dance it is the supplement of expressive gestures that lend the body's movement meaning. In other words, beyond what is visualized there exists a region that is implied. What moves here is understood to cause a trembling throughout the cobweb.

To bring these remarks back to the challenge of 'Hamlet's Mill': it appears that the aesthetic object is neither a field of interest coterminous with the universe nor a technologically innovative and purpose-engineered armature. It is a region or network, an ecosystem defined by shared interests. It is communication as communion. It blurs any distinction between the public and public space because it produces the space it inhabits by the character of its own motion. This twist in the argument might recall the passage in which the biologist D'Arcy Wentworth Thompson compared the erratic, seemingly random Brownian movement of unicellular creatures in a medium to the behavior of a human crowd. The key *restraint* on this comparison is that 'the bustling crowd has no *business* whatsoever.'[114] But this condition risks eliminating any explanatory value the simile might have. Unicellular creatures lack, we suppose, either introspection or intention. Their movements are determined by cohesive forces inherent in the medium. If human beings are going to form complex patterns redolent of turbulence, a mechanism of errancy must be found, a psycho-kinetic impulse that produces deviation from the straight line capable of producing the rotatory *folie à deux* of lovers.

In *Meeting Place* I suggest that René Girard's concept of 'mimetic desire' fulfills this role. According to Girard, 'one does not desire the other;

---

113 Marina Tsvetayeva, 'Tsvetayeva to Rilke, May 12, 1926' in Boris Pasternak, Marina Tsvetayeva, Rainer Maria Rilke, *Letters Summer 1926*, eds. Yevgeny Pasternak, Yelena Pasternak, K.M. Azadovsky, London: Jonathan Cape, 1986, 91.

114 See footnote 53 above.

desire for the other involves a third term, the "agent who serves as the 'model' or 'mediator' of the desire".[115] Transposed to the sociability induced by democracy's public space, Girard's 'agent' is something like the 'second skin' we spoke of earlier:

> ... the contrary impulses of attraction and repulsion that protect the personal spaces of the walkers are not simply pragmatic responses to the crowded conditions. They presuppose an invisible body toward which all are tending, and off whose flanks we continually rebound. This body is not a solid object, or even the idea of it: it is the space negotiated when it is perceived as public, as the strange attractor of those intent (ultimately) on meeting, even if meeting itself is always deferred. It is the public domain conceived as a crowd of third persons or desirous others, all going about their own business, which is the pursuit of an unattainable ideal. The sum of their motions is a volume, a hollow, a meeting place...[116]

In this case, the evolution of *turba* into *turbo*, which Correa and Correa recommend, can be reversed: it is the crowd (Latin *turba*) that grows turbulent. Such a crowd does not represent anything – that is not its business – but nevertheless it continuously produces form out of chaos, multiplying the opportunities for unpredictable encounter, without, it seems, any end in mind.

Claims have been made that these kinds of collective self-patterning can be observed and to some extent quantified. In 1919 the neo-Lamarckian biologist Paul Kammerer, published *Das Gesetz der Serie* (The Law of Seriality), whose typology of serial events was designed to explain the phenomenon of the 'mere coincidence.' When understood in relation to a theory of seriality, mere chance proves to be the manifestation of a

---

115 Carter, *Meeting Place*, 25.
116 Ibid., 27.

higher organizational principle, one characteristic of complex systems –
the anticipation of cybernetic models of systems-level self-organization
and growth is obvious:[117]

> Kammerer conducted many (rather naive) experiments, spending
> hours in parks noting occurrences of pedestrians with certain features
> (glasses, umbrellas, etc.) or in shops, noting precise times of arrivals
> of clients, and the like. Kammerer 'discovered' that the number of
> time intervals (of a fixed length) in which the number of objects under
> observation agrees with the average is much smaller than the number
> of intervals, where that number is either zero or larger than the
> average. This, he argued, provided evidence for clustering. From a stat-
> istician's point of view, clustering was an illusion of scale – from today's
> perspective, Kammerer merely noted the perfectly normal sponta-
> neous clustering of signals in the Poisson process.[118]

But as a chapter in the history of turbulence in performance, Kammerer's
speculations remain foundational. The new public of Vienna was neither
inanimate (ruled by an entirely unpredictable Brownian motion) nor
solely animated by conscious desire (Georg Simmel's lexicon of
metropolitan neurasthenias[119]): it was generating its own laws of seriality,
as in a performance letting the traces of sensory engagement penetrate
and begin to pattern the emerging identity of the work.

Feedback in this theory is not due to a prior psychological need – an

---

117 See John Townley and Robert Schmidt, 'Paul Kammerer and the Law of Seriality' for the
      influence of these ideas on the development of Jung's notion of 'synchronicity'. Both meditations
      occur in the context of the discoveries being made by physicists like Wolfgang Pauli which
      suggested that at the sub-atomic scale at least the position and the direction of a particle could
      not both be known at once: what you knew was inseparable from what you chose to know. See
      also Elena Nechita, 'Some Considerations on Seriality and Synchronicity,' BRAIN. Broad Research in
      Artificial Intelligence and Neuroscience 1, 1 (2010): 49-54.
118 Tomasz Downarowicz, 'Law of Series.' Accessed at www.scholarpedia.org/article/Law_of_series.
119 See Paul Carter, Repressed Spaces: the poetics of agoraphobia (London: Reaktion Books, 2002), 57.

affective disposition, say – but is the spontaneous (performative) enactment of a mimetic impulse. It is our love of copying that generates others whose multiplication and independence we cannot control. It seems logical that this chameleon-like interest in self-generation (or concealment) through the other will cause new types to appear, whose interests may well be 'Lamarckian' in the sense that they elevate the phenomenon of mere coincidence to an epigenetic mechanism. Two further contributors to 'On Turbulence,' Christian DuComb and Jessica Benmen, argue that turbulent human gatherings have a long history – traceable back to spontaneous political demonstrations. Such current phenomena as 'flash mobs' are under an illusion if they imagine themselves to be apolitical. The tradition of spontaneous crowd formations may, they suggest, be analogous to the physical phenomenon of hysteresis: something is left over, or becomes ingrained in society's communicational structures: a tendency to revolutionary chaos.[120] Turbulence is, in this sense, the patterning of these complex multiplicities; and the apt performance is the one that lets us see this. The designer of change is, in this context, the dramaturg of public space, the observer of 'mere coincidence' who values these instances of what Jung called synchronicity and aims to use them to educate ourselves about ourselves.

Obviously, this is not the world of the planner. It is ruled by the principle of like-to-like. Its realm is the middle ground of ceaseless human interaction and its information is stored in the informal choreographies that spiral inward and outwards through the medium of sociability. Communication in this place is metaphoric, that is, errant, wandering out of the path of true reason. Following a mimetic impulse comparable to Lucretius's *clinamen*, it constantly deviates. In psychological terms, it is under the aegis of *Ananke*, the 'errant principle of aimless necessity.'[121] The counterpart of this metaphysical principle in classical physics is

---

120 Christian DuComb and Jessica Benmen, 'Flash Mobs, Violence, and the Turbulent Crowd,' *Performance Research* 16, 5 (2014): 34-40.

121 James Hillman, *Re-visioning Psychology* (New York: Harper & Row, 1975), 159.

Democritus's notion of *peripalaisesthai* ('in any area of space, numerous particles are dancing aimlessly... ')[122] The mythic figure who finds a way through the turbulence is, according to James Hillman, Mercury or Hermes; his fictional counterpart is the Knight Errant, 'a mediator betwixt and between, homeless, of no fixed abode. Or his home, like that of Eros, is in the realm of the demons, of the metaxy (the middle region), in between, back and forth.'[123] Can anything be made, or made out, of this psychology, whether pursued individually or collectively? The vision of humanity it presents is certainly one of complex change, but can it be visualized? The artist of this world of chance is, according to Hillman, 'an odd-job man, a bricoleur... psychologizing upon and about what is at hand; not a systems architect, a planner with directions. And leaving, before completion, suggestion hanging in the air, an indirection, an open phrase... .'[124]

6. The Myth of the Meeting Place

Here we make the biggest leap. A new kind of research program, exploring the visualization of complexity, brings together arts and sciences. It is recognized that the patterning of data (information) reflects interests. A representationalist paradigm translates the sublime into easily digestible images of disaster; an alternative non-representationalist understanding of change seeks to incorporate the turbulence-producing phenomenon of feedback into the research method. Perhaps there is a relationship between the designer of complexity and the dramaturg of the crowd. The figure/ground distinction between aesthetic object and context dissolves. It is replaced by the community of interest, the region of the in-between – the

---

122 Jonathan Barnes, *The Presocratic Philosophers* (London: Routledge, 1983), 366.

123 Hillman, *Re-visioning Psychology*, 161.

124 Ibid., 164.

Involute 7, artline texta 0.4 on paper, 148 x 210 mm, March 2005. A36, 203.

54

inter esse – defined by a certain nomadic propensity. The nomads are not lost: they have tracks: they are driven by a mimetic desire that carves out a densifying scratch field of lines (attractions, collisions, deviations and revisions). As self-conscious subjects, they act out the phenomenon of turbulence. Their desirous economy is restless but strangely disinterested – not uninterested but driven by a contextual curiosity that has almost Lamarckian feel to it. We want to change: therefore we will change. In this guise the new creative community is no longer a voice of humanistic conscience, crying out against the anthropogenic alteration of the biosphere. It is the secret sharer of changes in which it colludes: how can employees of creativity cry out against the greatest change of all, the modification of global living conditions?

If the meeting place is not to be an analog of ceaseless movement but a site of public education, it has to seize hold of the rules of engagement. These are not reducible to the free fall of desire. The catalyst of change in Girard's model of mimetic desire, the agent, is not an empirical object: he, she or it is a myth, a symbolic form that focuses the meaning of life on the pursuit of what lies beyond. It is the myth, the symbolic concentration (dramaturgy, we might say) of discourse that regionalizes or patterns the *peripalaisesthai* of random movements, and their human corollary, the frisson of erotic encounter. The myth is not simply a story (a parable) that ably condenses or metaphorizes a diversity of phenomena under a plausible unifying psychological hypothesis. It is the *topos*, or narrative formation where new meanings are made possible. As a mouthing, or performative mode of communication, mythic sense-making is the science of the meeting place. The paradoxical myth of modernity, enshrined in the behaviorist conception of sociability contained in the planner's directions, is that the meeting place is voiceless and shapeless – that, without the Creationist planner, it lacks the capacity to generate the hither and thither of discourse.

The radical step at this juncture of our discussion of the design of turbulence is to consider that the designer is a poet, or, if not a poet, a rhapsode, a channeller of those stories that, adapted to the concrete situation of the community, can link the act of recollection to the task of invention. In the long gestation of the research program known as 'Hamlet's Mill,' the mythological reference of the name fell under increasingly acute scrutiny. It came to be felt that the thesis of Santillana and von Dechend's book, *Hamlet's Mill*, offered a less than rigorous analysis of mythological data. These authors had noted that, according to one Norse saga attributed to Snorri, 'the whirlpool came into being from the unhinging of the Grotte Mill: the Maelstrom comes of the hole in the sunken millstone.' That is, the whirlpool forms where water falls through the hole in the millstone.[125] Why is the Grotte 'unhinged'? Santillana and von Dechend explain that *Grotte* does not mean millstone but axle-block, the round block of wood which fills the hole in the millstone. The 'grotte' 'created a hole when the mill tree sprang out of it, and the whirlpool formed in the hole.'[126] But how did that happen? Simply by plunging into the sea? The authors establish the identity of the mill with 'heaven';[127] then, with the observation of the precession of the equinoxes in mind, argue that 'The unhinging of the Mill is caused by the shifting of the world axis.'[128]

This thesis, that the Norse original of Shakespeare's equivocating Hamlet was ultimately a figure who managed the first great event of global climate change, was thought likely to meet with what Mircea Eliade refers to as 'the disfavor and failure of the man "without imagination"... .'[129] As these men (mostly), imaginatively challenged or not, populated the bureaucracies most likely to support the development of the project, the identification of it with a remarkable, but nevertheless eccentric, mythopoetic caprice, was judged to be needlessly provocative. In 2004 Professor Steven Connor (then of Birkbeck College) and I had applied for a Leverhulme Grant called 'Waterlogs: Matter, Making, Thinking,' 'a

---

125 De Santillana and von Dechend, *Hamlet's Mill*, 90.
126 Ibid., 91.
127 Ibid., 141.
128 Ibid., 147.
129 Mircea Eliade, *Images and Symbols*, 20.

linked series of projects and commissions into the importance of water as material form, circumstance and environment.' The application explained, 'Our point of focus will be London and the ways in which the water of the Thames, and the sea to which it gives access, has shaped, determined and entered into the cultural life of the capital and nation.' And we clarified that 'Our emphasis will not be directly on the biology or physics or politics of water, so much as on what might be called the "material imagination" of water – its role as a model for, and stimulus to, thinking, and the invention of metaphor. We will be interested in particular to uncover through historical thought and discover for creative work the ways in which water allows apprehension of blendings, compoundings, dissolutions, soft edges, and mixed conditions.'[130]

Already at that stage a connection was proposed between the mythopoetic imagination and the regeneration of the public domain. When James I threatened to remove the Court to the country, the City of London merchants retorted that, while he might retire, he could not take the river with him – which is to say that the foundation of London's well-being was the communication that the river made possible. In the same spirit 'Waterlogs' located the creative imagination of the city in its largest public space, the river. Already I had contributed to the notes for this project 'Wordcoil,' a proposal to create a waterspout structure in the Tate Modern's Turbine Hall – I had been surprised that the transformation of the old power station for the purposes of commissioning and displaying modern and contemporary art had eliminated all allusion to the rotatory sources of power it previously housed. A year later I was recasting this as 'Hamlet's Mill,' and at the invitation of the Chair of the Olympic Culture and Education Committee for London 2012, contemplating the development of a design concept that might be included in the London Olympics 2012 Public Art Program.

---

130   Steven Connor and Paul Carter, 'Waterlogs: Matter, Making, Thinking,' London Consortium application to Leverhulme Trust, 2004, 1-6, 1. In author's possession.

In this heroic phase we managed to obtain start-up venture capital and, reminding our stakeholders that 'In myth Shakespeare's Hamlet is the Turner of the World and the Master of the Whirlpool. He twirls the Axis of the Globe,' we outlined:

> a major public artwork sited on the edge of the Thames adjacent to The Globe Theatre and the Tate Modern... A giant pivot, or gate post which appears to rotate. Its rate of rotation is directly related to the rate of global climate change. As it rotates with greater or lesser speed, the 'ribbons' from which it is formed unwind. The cultural allusion is to the May Dance, itself a traditional art form celebrating the relationship between the sustaining of life and the order of the universe. We would like the 'ribbons' to be programmable surfaces through which electronic text can run; the technology for this exists, but its application in a watery environment will require further investigation. The work's turning incorporates, poetically, allusions to the Bankside turbine, the Globe Theatre, but, using wave and wind generated energy to produce its effects, also reflects critically on anthropocentric attitudes to the environment.[131]

In the event this vision proved impossible to sustain. It is introduced here in the context of understanding the role of myth in place-making. In this phase of the project we remained attached to a figure/ground notion of the relationship between our 'climate change myth' and the place where it was to be located. When this high tide of funding optimism began to recede, we remained committed to building a change monitor, but our conception of its relation to the environment had changed. By then the Environment Agency had released its 2100 Thames Tidal Flood Management Report, which had recommended a gradualist approach to

---

131 Material Thinking, 'Hamlet's Mill: Measuring Global Warming in London,' 1-12. 10 September 2006. Available from author.

the management of flood risk, one where the flood plain and its associated wetlands were accommodated and micromanaged – rather than being pre-emptively drained and bulwarked. But it was acknowledged that good communication with the public was essential to the viability of this strategy. In raising awareness not only of risk but of opportunity, the engagement of creative communities and of public artists seemed obvious. In one proposal we mooted, the new 'Hamlet's Mill' 'would be distributed across the 20-odd boroughs. A mother-ship (mother board?) might be located bobbing on the water opposite Greenwich or the Millennium Dome but it would have faces or interfaces via subsidiary nodes, portals or performance spaces in every borough. In short, an archipelago work of some kind.'[132]

The figure/ground distinction was dissolving. Steven Connor had already expressed doubts about the Santillana/Dechene thesis and the capacity of the name 'Hamlet's Mill' to communicate the full scope of the endeavour. A leading scholar of Michel Serres's work, Connor had drawn our attention to Serres' concept of *syrrhesis*, suggesting we needed to reconceptualize the work, less as a freestanding armature and far more as a creative process involving the public in a new orientation to the land/water world they inhabited. In response I acknowledged that our name placed emphasis on the wrong part of the Hamlet myth: it was not the antediluvian machine that was of most interest but the diluvian response and postdiluvian stabilisation of the flux – not Hamlet the Miller but the proto-Shakespearean post-Deluge Hamlet, who was charged with managing turbulence – and who, transposed to our epoch, finds that 'To become or not to become' is the question. For change is inevitable: the only question is how it will be understood, narrated and designed. In this context, I noted that Serres's definition of *syrrhesis* bore some resemblance to the connotations of the English word flood. Obviously *rhesis* and flood share the idea of flow or fluency. Flood is associated with *flodus* meaning a

---

132 Material Thinking, 'Hamlet's Name: evoking the Flood,' 1-3. July 2010.

river. It is also associated with the word 'fleet' meaning a number of ships. The meanings of flood imply, then, movement and the mastery of movement. Interestingly, in his cultural history of the Mediterranean, Matvejevic derives the Serb word for island from a root meaning to drift.[133] In any case, the topology of a design project directed towards the communication of complex change might look more like the navigation of an archipelago in which all parts moved in relation to all other parts.

Poetic genealogies of this kind attempt to ground the method of the project in the mapping of relationships. They suggest that the great divide in contemporary research programs between quantitatively and qualitatively based methodologies rests on an impoverished idea of both. It is significant that our word *relate* applies equally to the scientific ambition to make sense of things and to the ambition of language, and especially myth, to tell stories. Narrative is not an analog of linear thinking: in metaphoric thinking, one thing does not lead to another. Instead, the likenesses that poetic thinking perceives between unlike things draw them together: two tracks approach each other down curving paths. In other words, ideation itself may have a helical form, resembling the operation of a turbine. London, to return to the amplified public space of our project, might in the visualization of complex change look more like a page from Descartes's celestial mechanics than a conventional map. Its dramaturgy might be a construction of vortices. This is not only a speculation about the topology of topics – the way narratives curl in upon themselves – but may have a persuasive cultural signature. Above all, it suggests an approach to the visualization of complex data sets that integrates observation and interest, and which grounds metaphorical modes of understanding firmly in the behavior of crowds, or swarms, whose collective behaviors are sublime.

A turbulent London is not, then, such a far-fetched dream. It might be the mythopoetic form of a collective consciousness, the city when the

133 Predrag Matvejevic, *Mediterranean Breviary: A Cultural Landscape*, trans. M.H. Heim (Oakland, CA: University of California Press, 1999).

informe of large data sets (the endless evolutionary fluctuations of its Brownian Movement) becomes, through the feedback of conscious reaction information, a communication of common choice and purpose. Kevin Cope observes how the quintessential poetic observer of London life, John Gay, 'is wholeheartedly vortectical. His heart a helix, he perceives the world as a spiral. The poet of the periphery, he never walks down the centre of the streets, preferring to wander along alleyways – to shimmy towards his destination, the centre of the city.'[134] His 'periphery' is 'a ray defined by its motion from the city and its encounter with centre-seeking viewers. And a turbulent encounter it is: like pencils drawing spirals, Gay's circulating but centripetal citizens are always on a roll.'[135] Thomas de Quincey, another habitué of London's nocturnal streets, internalizes the city, observing, 'The fleeting accidents of a man's life, and its external shows, may indeed be irrelate and incongruous; but the organizing principles which fuse into harmony, and gather about fixed predetermined centres, whatever heterogeneous elements life may have accumulated from without, will not permit the grandeur of human unity greatly to be violated.'[136] Grasped positively, though, the 'organizing principles' produce 'involutes' – 'far more of our deepest thoughts and feelings pass to us through perplexed combinations of *concrete* objects, pass to us as *involutes* (if I may coin that word) in compound experiences incapable of being disentangled, than ever reach us *directly*, and in their own abstract states.'[137]

As regards the mythmaker, the dramaturg of the maelstrom – the new urban designer of information – De Quincey writes that the involute can be compared to a 'map' and the guide through its perplexities is the

---

134 Kevin L. Cope, 'Spinning Descartes into Blake: Spirals, Vortices, and the Dynamics of Deviation,' in *Spiral Symmetry*, ed. I. Hargittai & C.A. Pickover (Singapore: World Scientific, 2000), 415.

135 Ibid., 416.

136 Thomas de Quincey, 'The Palimpsest of The Human Brain,' *Suspiria de Profundis*, Accessed at https://ebooks.adelaide.edu.au/d/de_quincey/thomas/suspiria-de-profundis/chapter2.html.

137 Ibid.

hermetic figure of the Dark Interpreter, a *hypnogogus* whose power of association is clearly erotic, who is an 'apparition… but a reflex of yourself' – 'in uttering your secret feelings to him, you make this phantom the dark symbolic mirror for reflecting to the daylight what else must be hidden forever.'[138] The Dark Interpreter could also be the Change Monitor, the form of 'Hamlet's Mill' emerging out of his dark symbolic mirror. Like Hermes with his serpent-entwined caduceus, he is the hypnogogue of deviation, whose natural writing style is the arabesque, the revolving line that never becomes concentric but wobbles, like the earth's axis, or, to put it another way, quoting another London author, John Donne, 'nor can the Sunne/ Perfit a Circle, or maintaine his way/ One inch direct; but where he rose to-day/ He comes no more, but with a couzening line,/ Steales by that point, and so is Serpentine… So, of the Starres which boast that they doe runne/ In Circle still, none ends where he begun… .'[139] This also describes the route of spiritual ascent – Donne writes of the supplicant's tearful approach to God in Sermons V as 'a religious insinuation, and a circumvention that God loves.' It is 'to gather upon God by a rolling Trench, and by a winding staire' and is an act 'of the wisedome of the Serpent, which our Saviour recommends unto us, in such a *Serpentine* line, (as the Artists call it) to get up to God… .'[140]

Such cultural arabesques as these may inform the design of 'Hamlet's Mill.' They may also throw light on Hamlet and the manner of his appearance. Artists have interpreted the phrase 'mortal coil' incorrectly, it seems, as a rope-like coil, when it may have some sense of 'crowd, hubbub, noise' (perhaps from the French verb *cueillir* – to gather or lay together). In this case the double spiral is the analogue of democratic public space where people gather and mingle without any other business.

---

138 Ibid.

139 John Donne, 'The First Anniversary, An Anatomy of the World,' lines 268-277. Accessed at http://www.bartleby.com/357/169.html

140 L.E. Semler, *The English Mannerist Poets and the Visual Arts* (Madison, NJ: Fairleigh Dickinson University Press, 1998), 50.

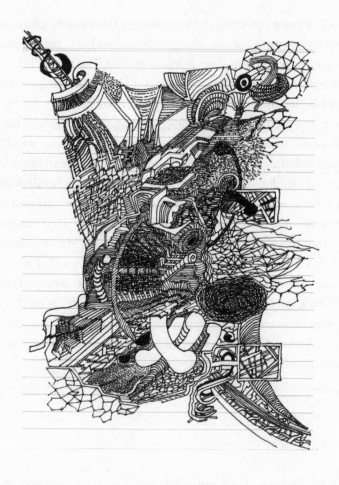

Involute 8, artline texta 0.4 on paper, 148 x 210 mm, August 2005. A36, 261.

Turbulence is not an unforeseen by-product of the meeting-place but the distinguishing feature of its design. Some writers have found in Shakespeare's plays, and in their primum mobile, The Globe Theatre, an elaborate system of micro-macro-analogies. Isn't The Globe a kind of massive mill, its upper and lower storeys corresponding to the two millstones? The master of the 'O,' the open stage, is Shakespeare. Isn't this what his name means, he that catches the axle tree and steadies its gyroscopic wobbling? These kinds of analogy can be extended to the maelstrom of Hamlet's indecision. His entire psychology revolves around the choice between an act of revenge that will bring down his soul and an act of revenge that will bring him back to the light. He is suspended between the opposed inclinations. But, apparently, this psychological condition has a physical counterpart. I discover that 'vortical motion' in 'turbulence' produces 'double spiral vortex layers wrapped around tubular vortex cores.'[141] In this vortical reading, Hamlet is stuck on the winding stair of becoming. However, his dramaturgical role is clear: like Mercury in Botticelli's *La Primavera*, his job is to drive the clouds along, to stir up and monitor complex change.

7. The Governor

Feedback is a feature of self-organizing systems; some, but not all, self-organizing systems grow more complex. This is an important distinction sociologically as well as cybernetically. It explains how institutionalized research programs are usually unable to incorporate the organization of physical reality into their model of the research program. The centrifugal governor used in James Watt's steam engines serves to minimize turbulence

---

141   Shigeo Kida, 'Life, Structure, and Dynamical Role of Vortical Motion in Turbulence.' Accessed at
      http://www.igf.fuw.edu.pl/iutam/ABSTRACTS/Kida.pdf

(dissipation, energy loss). James Clerk Maxwell's paper on the mathematics of governors is rightly characterized as an early contribution to control theory. A closed system of this kind maintains itself through a self-corrective circuit (the feedback mechanism). However, in more complex systems, feedback produces change as well as continuity: 'Data about the system's previous actions, as a part of the input it receives, is monitored, allowing the system to "watch" itself, and thus signal the degree of attainment or non-attainment of a given operation relative to pre-established goals. This process allows a system to alter its output and thereby regulate or steer its behavior in relation to its pre-encoded goals. Thus, two forms of feedback are recognized, negative and positive.'[142]

I mention these well-known features, common to technological and biological systems, in order to highlight the eccentricity of the conditions under which publicly-funded research programs are expected to operate. In these the different controls (legal, financial and administrative) have as their goal the maintenance of pre-encoded goals. The research program has, almost by definition, if its object is the study of change, to be flexible. To attend to emergent data, it must monitor its own performance and adapt to circumstance. Its principal data are, in fact, evidence of positive feedback – mismatches between 'the system's actual behavior and its intended performance.'[143] However, it is precisely these 'new horizons', at once phenomenological and methodological, that the State through its research funding agencies aims to control and regulate. Following their political masters, the universities act as governors regulating creativity. Negative feedback is, as we know, maintained at the cost of the growing destabilization of the context; where 'exchange' between the system and its environment is curtailed or repressed, a differential pressure grows that eventually leads to the system's collapse. A good example of this in Australian research culture is the divorce of the humanities and social

---

142 Lawrence S. Bale, 'Gregory Bateson, Cybernetics, and the Social/Behavioural Sciences,' 15.
www.narberthpa.com/Bale/lsbale_dop/gbcatsbs.pdf
143 Ibid.

sciences from the design disciplines; and the separation of both of these, when framing research programs, from 'forming situations' in the real world where the complexification of relationships fuses problem and outcome into a single dynamic process of symbolic formation.

In another place it will be necessary to examine the historical roots of this extraordinary institutional survival of 'second law paranoia.'[144] Here the point is merely that the kind of research program adumbrated in a creative interdisciplinary community is, paradoxically, threatening to the institutional culture notionally supportive of the individual forming that community. Thus, it is hard not to agree with Riedl when he comments,

> The use of linear causality seems to me the main obstacle to dealing adequately with complex systems. Industries and business have fostered it for too long. It is, besides greed, the main cause of the environmental problem. It is not yet fully seen that complexity needs a more elaborated causality concept.[145]

But the logic of corporate self-interest is not confined to the public sector: it defines second-order bureaucracy where the managers employed to monitor the 'systems' put in place secondary systems that secure their own survival, even though this second-order regulation ultimately kills the host (the learning and research community).

Quantitative investigations of complexity might seem to be immune to these human foibles; however, it is undeniable that all turbulence specialists, economists, meteorologists, nano-technologists, software designers and even biologists, occupy niches within a research ecology

---

144 With reference to the proposition that entropy always increases, contradicted by the 'anti-entropic evidence in the evolution of order and increased complexity within biological systems [which] simply cannot be explained with traditional liner concepts such as the second law of thermodynamics.' Ibid., 6.

145 Rupert Riedl in *Darwinism & Philosophy*, ed. Vittorio Hösle and Christian Illies (Indiana: University of Notre Dame Press, 2005), 141.

not of their making. To a large extent perceived success in this environment depends on cultivating an invulnerability to change: the cellular walls between disciplines are rarely breached. The pursuit of quantification has marginalized the value of qualification; dissection rules at the expense of relation – 'Perhaps the most damaging result of over-specialization in scientific inquiry is that it has obstructed the perception and study of the non-substantial phenomena intrinsically manifest in relationships.'[146] In contrast with the vortical descent into the phenomenon of turbulence, which overwhelms borders or discourses of verification established between disciplines, our universities perpetuate feedback loops whose 'circuitry' is closed, and whose innovations therefore tend to be an intensification of the same. When Donald Verene complains, 'Memory is forgotten by the modern world as our attempt to release hope points us toward the future. The future for the modern world is the present made more extreme,' he does not simply refer to history.[147] He has in mind the mythopoetic genesis of the new, which, in other terms, is the 'positive feedback' of a culture that understands its 'fictions' as creative algorithms. To narrate change in a way that avoids relating (and relating to) change is to inhabit a vicious circle.

Fictions are relations, and our relationship to them is critical to the way we imagine the governance of research. We can use them as governors to increase our power whilst maintaining the status quo. Or we can use them to restore lost relations with the world, in the manner of Michael Tawa's ana-materialism – a marriage of phenomenological principles of analysis to the inherent indeterminism of complex systems whose behavior is – like the approach he recommends to design – non-linear, that is, both scripturally and ethically, open, unfinished, receptive to innovation.[148] The institutional myth of research corresponds to Vaihinger's 'as if' theory of

---

146 Bale, 'Gregory Bateson, Cybernetics, and the Social/Behavioural Sciences,' 6.

147 Donald Verene, *Philosophy and the Return to Self Knowledge* (Hew Haven, Conn: Yale University Press, 1991, 198.

148 Michael Tawa, *Theorising the Project* (Newcastle, UK: Cambridge Scholars Press, 2011), 236.

psychic conservation. Elsewhere I have applied this model to the mindset of the colonizer, whose physical conquest of the world reproduces externally what the 'as if' development of the psyche achieves internally.[149] Here its application to the theory and practice of research management is relevant. The character of the individual psyche, he writes, applies equally to the collective mindset: 'the psyche is a machine that is continuously improving itself, and whose purpose is to perform as safely, expeditiously and with the minimum expenditure of energy, the movement necessary for the preservation of the organism; movements in the broadest sense of the word, as the ultimate objectives of all our acts.'[150] To become a 'thought machine,' the psyche develops a system of pulleys and levers. These mechanisms connect 'sense-complexes' by creating 'fixed nuclei.' These devices can be compared to 'fictions' or 'provisional abstractions,' and once established act as 'similarity centres' allowing sensations derived from the external world to be provisionally categorized and ordered. Obviously there is feedback here: the 'as if' achievement of the psyche evolves to meet the challenge of navigating the external world. At the same time, the psyche imagined like this engulfs the world. In cybernetic terms, its purpose is to impose negative feedback wherever it goes.

The significance of these observations is not confined to the sociology of research programs. It is not simply the sideways conversations between different parts of the 'system' that matter if the character of complexity is to be communicated, but the goals of the research that are implicated. When Correa and Correa state, 'An idea is wrong if it cannot account for the relationships it seeks to establish, explain and condense; if it decontextualizes the relation,'[151] they refer to the qualitative, or aesthetic (in Jorn's broadest sense), aspect of research. They attack the 'as if' model of research, the idea that fictions or hypotheses are purely intellectual stepping stones that serve

---

149   Paul Carter, *The Lie of the Land* (London: Faber & Faber, 1996), 234-235.
150   Hans Vaihinger, *The Philosophy of 'As If': A System of the Theoretical, Practical and Religious Fictions*, trans. C.K. Ogden (London: Routledge and Kegan Paul, 1924), 101.
151   Correa and Correa, 'Whither Science?,' 41.

(ultimately) to reinforce the sovereignty of the thinking subjects. They ask for a research culture that exists in an ethical relationship with its environment. Translated into the terms of 'Hamlet's Mill,' they identify the key issue in the visualization of complex data sets as ethical or, rather, as one where the aesthetic and the ethical have to fuse. A fiction is unavoidable. It is the condition of making sense but, if it is fully to make sense, it must be able to communicate an awareness of what it communicates – to relate to what it relates. Most representations of scientific data, including *An Inconvenient Truth*, fail this criterion. To put it another way, to make sense of things, the researcher needs to cultivate a sensibility.

In this context, Vaihinger's 'provisional abstractions' might be compared with Arakawa and Gins' 'tentative constructed plans... useful for guiding an exact positioning of the elements that should, in our estimation, when all put precisely in place, yield some type of palpable sensibility.'[152] The 'landing places' that Arakawa and Gins propose to make are perceptions of the world. They materialize the site, rather than treat it as an 'as if' fiction. It is a fiction of a different kind, one that takes account of what happens, the event, which, as an encounter in passing 'might be the cleaving of energymatter.'[153] It is not a phenomenological stance: a theory of creativity is foreshadowed: 'forming space, the perceiving brings about the perceived image of fiction of place as detail; by repeatedly cleaving, it initiates the game of distance, making it possible, for example, for one's arm, hand or foot to be seen.'[154] Obviously the tactics of a new art practice should not be compared directly with a late nineteenth century theory of scientific discovery. But common to both formulations is a shadowing concept of feedback. In the case of Arakawa and Gins we have the kernel of an approach to the kind of research program that 'Hamlet's Mill' might be: a proprioceptive choreography is suggested, a complexification of

---

152 Arakawa and Madeline Gins, 'The Tentative Constructed Plan as Intervening Device (for a Reversible Destiny),' unpublished typescript, 1-8.
153 Ibid., 3.
154 Ibid.

human behavior through 'Viewing the human body as site (for action, but also for construction... of the perceived world).' Education – communication of complexity – would occur when it became palpable that the 'site' is 'ubiquitous.' At this point the ethical and the aesthetic fuse.

8. Parametric Parables

Leonardo da Vinci's already quoted observation about non-laminar flow suggested that complexity might be usefully visualized in the form of turbulence. But it also gave a clue – at least to the genius of James Clerk Maxwell – to how turbulence might be mathematicised. Theoretical physicists may think it a case of special pleading to claim for Maxwell a modest place in the history of English language Scottish poetry but the formulation of the differential equations that demonstrated electricity, magnetism and light were different manifestations of one phenomenon owed something to his *metaphoric* gift. Maxwell 'relied on two key mathematical operations for analyzing a field to reveal its charge and current structure': 'convergence' and 'curl.' Both were applied to a point in the field. Convergence measured 'the extent to which the field was aimed at the point'; 'curl' 'measured the rotational character of the field at the point.'[155]

Maxwell explained his decision to 'call this vector the Curl or Version of the original vector function': 'I have sought a word which shall neither, like Rotation, Whirl, or Twirl, connote motion, nor, like Twist, indicate a helical or screw structure which is not of the vector at all.'[156] Curl represented a new parameter in the modeling of a phenomenon, a new

---

155 William H. Cropper, *Great Physicists: The Life and Time of Leading Physicists from Galileo to Hawking* (Oxford: Oxford University Press, 2004), 161.

156 James Clerk Maxwell, 'Remarks on the Mathematical Classification of Physical Quantities,' *Proceedings of the London Mathematical Society*, s1-3, 1871, 224-233, 233.

Involute 9, artline texta 0.4 on paper, 148 x 210 mm, January 2006. A36, 338.

constant whose variability provided information about the state of the 'flux.' It was in this sense simply another physical concept that could be quantified. It was, however, something more, an extraordinary conceptualization of the curvilinear constitution of electromagnetic phenomena. Curl was not an effect of motion: it expressed the idea that space consisted of 'a sea of molecular vortices,' that 'Each whirlpool is in fact a tiny electric circuit.'[157] Or, as Sir Oliver Lodge wrote, 'Maxwell perceived that a magnetic field was wrapped around a current, and that a current could equally well be wrapped around a magnetic field, that in fact the relation between them was reciprocal, and could be expressed mathematically by what he subsequently called *curl*.'[158]

Convergence and curl were constants that could, as it were, enable calculations or predictions that took the chaotic turbulence out of vortical motion. Maxwell was influenced in his conceptualization of the electromagnetic field by observations he had made of the dynamics of fluids. He was interested in the parameters of a circular whirlpool that determined whether its motion was stable or unstable. His equations suggested how turbulence could be managed. In the other direction, however, his taxonomy of vectors made possible the study of instability or 'endogenously erratic dynamics.' It is notable that the man who 'developed the theoretical unification of electricity and magnetism' was also amongst the first to consider the 'sensitive dependence on initial conditions' 'characteristic of chaotically dynamic nonlinear systems.' Aware of 'that class of phenomena such that a spark kindles a forest, a rock creates an avalanche or a word prevents an action,' Maxwell appreciated how a small change in a dynamical system could generate much larger

---

157 Frederick David Tombe, 'The Significance of Maxwell's Equations,' 6 at http://freenrg.info/ Physics/Frederick_David_Tombe/tombe77.pdf

158 Tapan K. Sarkar et al., 'Who Was James Clerk Maxwell and What Was/Is His Electromagnetic Theory?,' at http://www.ieeeaps.org/sarkar.pdf

changes.[159] Similarly, Maxwell's 1868 paper 'On Governors' may be 'a classic in feedback control theory'[160] but the 'dynamical theory'[161] developed to explain how the centrifugal governor used in steam engines works arises in response to the phenomenon of turbulent steam.

Maxwell's concept of curl enables him to fix a parameter, but it is arrived at parabolically, through the roundabout route of analogy. With something like the exactitude of Leonardo's analogy – comparing the turbulent flow of water to curls of hair – Maxwell visualizes a critical feature of the vector field: working from the analogy of vortical motion in water, he proposes a critical constant that makes the visualization of another 'dynamical system' possible. A parameter is a constant that allows a changing field to be measured or modeled. A parable is another kind of measure, a comparison thrown alongside in a way that brings out the character of the situation. Both involve a creative cut into the flux of time and space, and both exist in relation to the flux or field that exceeds their efforts at control. In exceptional circumstances there may be a fit between the phenomenon and the thing laid alongside it. Then there is control and measure. But this is a moment of reflexivity or coincidence between mental and physical world that is exceptional. As Michel Serres states, 'Save for exceptional instances, we perceive almost nothing of this intense chaos which nonetheless exists and functions, as experiments have demonstrated conclusively.'[162]

The feedback that interests Maxwell for practical purposes is essential to the maintenance of a system's steady state, but it is also the mechanism of potentially non-homeostatic change: as Bale summarizes,

159   J. Barkley Rosser, 'Chaos Theory before Lorenz,' 2008. 'Turbulence is any chaotic solution to the Navier-Stokes equations that is sensitive to initial data... ' Chapman & Tobak, quoted by J.M. McDonough, 'Introductory Lectures on Turbulence', 5, at www.engr.uky.edu/~acfd/lctr-notes634.pdf

160   Wikipedia 'Centrifugal Governor.'

161   James Clerk Maxwell, 'On Governors,' Proceedings of the Royal Society, No. 100 (1868), 1-12, 1.

162   Serres, 'The Origin of Language: Biology, Information Theory, & Thermodynamics.'

Cybernetic research has convincingly demonstrated that through the deviation- amplifying mutual causal process of positive feedback, starting anywhere except the thermo-dynamically most probable equilibrium, open systems will complexify in response to enduring perturbations from the environment. In short, 'whenever a lasting deviation from uniformity (thermodynamic equilibrium) develops,' a system will move toward increased differentiation and complexification, and therefore, a more tenuous steady state. It will adapt itself to environmental conditions by altering and complexifying its organization, and increased complexification in all natural systems represents movement away from systemic stability.[163]

In other words, 'as a system's configuration becomes more intricately organized and more intimately interrelated with increased external variables, it becomes more sensitive and responsive to change, and thereby less stable. However, the emergence of increased differentiation and complexification also manifests a corresponding increase in the system's array of available responses, or what Ervin Laszlo terms cybernetic stability – the system's capacity for effective adaptation.'[164] Cybernetic stability in this context means the internalization of feedback as a self-organizational principle. Described here is a model of differentiation and growth that overcomes the traditional figure/ground or culture/environment divide. Its biological equivalent would by C.H. Waddington's 'epigenetic landscape,' where a cell may take divergent developmental paths (chreodes) under different conditions. The point is that such alterations are not random but occur in a strict feedback loop with environmental constraints.[165]

---

163 Bale, 'Gregory Bateson, Cybernetics, and the Social/Behavioural Sciences.'
164 Ibid.
165 For summary and discussion, see Scott F. Gilbert, 'Diachronic Biology Meets Evo-Devo: C.H. Waddington's Approach to Evolutionary Biology,' *Integrative & Comparative Biology* 40, 5 (2000): 729-737. Accessed at http://icb.oxfordjournals.org/content/40/5/729.full

The genius of Maxwell is partly to arrive at mathematically quantifiable parameters parabolically – by analogies from observation that are computable. He is able to conceptualise complex dynamic systems because he is able to see what determines complexity. The intrusion of a poetic hypothesis to explain Maxwell's science is not to diminish or mystify his gift for symbolic logic. It is to foreground the fact that his research obeyed a feedback law of verification. But for the existence of an unknowable complexity simplification would be impossible. The task of the theoretical physicist is to discern patterns or designs informing the mesh of reality that are unknown to the parts that inform the whole. The power to transcend a merely empirical verification of phenomena depends on the observer transcending his own ego and being able to listen, as it were, to information coming back from Nature as a result of his parametric modeling.

In his poem, 'Reflex Musings: Reflections from Various Surfaces,' Maxwell compares this process to walking through a crowd:

In the dense entangled street,
Where the web of Trade is weaving,
Forms unknown in crowds I meet
Much of each and all believing;
Each his small designs achieving
Hurries on with restless feet,
While, through Fancy's power deceiving,
Self in every form I greet.

This cryptic reflection is amplified in the following verses:

Oft in yonder rocky dell
Neath the birches' shadow seated,
I have watched the darksome well,
Where my stooping form, repeated,

75

Now advanced and now retreated
With the spring's alternate swell,
Till destroyed before completed
As the big drops grew and fell.
By the hollow mountain-side
Questions strange I shout for ever,
While the echoes far and wide
Seem to mock my vain endeavour;
Still I shout, for though they never
Cast my borrowed voice aside,
Words from empty words they sever—
Words of Truth from words of Pride.

Yes, the faces in the crowd,
And the wakened echoes, glancing
From the mountain, rocky browed,
And the lights in water dancing—
Each my wandering sense entrancing,
Tells me back my thoughts aloud,
All the joys of Truth enhancing
Crushing all that makes me proud.[166]

Nature shatters the mirror of narcissistic or solipsistic thought – the kind of thinking that fancies the Self reflected everywhere. Unlike D'Arcy Wentworth Thompson's crowd, which pursues 'no *business* whatsoever,' Maxwell's is busily employed in weaving the web of trade. In other respects, though, its 'Forms unknown' are, like Thompson's 'Brownian movement,' images of turbulence. These 'Forms unknown' can be compared to algorithms, equations that represent generative patterns

---

166 Accessed at http://www.poemhunter.com/best-poems/james-clerk-maxwell/reflex-musings-
reflections-from-various-surfaces/

informing the 'small designs' but undetectable to the individual. Algorithmically-set parameters allow the field to be stretched, warped, expanded and contracted. Provided the topological characteristics of the field remain the same, the 'web of Trade' can spread, retract, regroup and diffuse as the numerical values put into the parameters are changed. The analogy with human and animal behavior is compelling. When, for example, Peter Miller describes 'a smart swarm' as 'a group of individuals who respond to one another and their environment in ways that give them the power, as a group, to cope with complexity and change,'[167] he evokes a crowd that is parametrically organized or self-aware. In another register such a crowd is parabolically organized, able to lie beside itself as it were; for what is thrown alongside, the outline that suggests a form unknown, becomes the determinant of the group's anonymous, but nevertheless purposeful, swarming. Another 'On Turbulence' contributor, James Riley, to whom I owe the reference to Peter Miller, discusses the phenomenon of 'multi-sited protests' that characterize contemporary demonstrations. As an instance of 'the extensive use of "digitalized and networked modalities" [to] supplement an *in situ* embodiment by permitting the wide diffusion of a symbolic statement and a theoretically unofficial flow of real-time information,' he cites Anonymous, 'the first internet-based superconsciousness,' which exists as a group 'in the sense that a flock of birds is a group,' but which, just as birds can act autonomously within the flock, may also remain diffuse and centreless.[168]

The methodology of a research project aimed at the visualization of complexity depends on an intuition of reciprocity between the data under investigation and the interests of the observer. There exists a middle ground between the tendency of dynamical systems to grow more complex and the pattern-making propensity of human beings. It is the existence of this middle ground that lends sense to what the senses

---

167 Peter Miller, *Smart Swarm* (London: Collins, 2010), xvi.
168 James Riley, 'Insect Traffic: Protest, Activism and the Swarm,' *Performance Research* 16, 5 (2014): 41-48, 43.

vouchsafe us. It is the medium of 'connections that function' whose pursuit and recognition is a source of 'active joy.' It is in this sense that Mark Burry advocates 'simplexity' in the field of digital scripting. In supporting 'an idea being propagated in the mind and substantially worked into a design through purely intellectual processes,' he is not advocating over-simplification. Rather, he is warning against the uncritical use of computationally generative processes that produce 'complexification' without obvious value. He is urging a hybrid method in which an intuition of emergent form and an algorithmic inventiveness make possible the appearance of 'Forms unknown' that we yet recognize as an improvement.[169] In a similar vein, as we saw, Correa & Correa maintain that, 'The real challenge of science is its minor becoming, but in the precise sense of a search for the functions, the energy functions, which create the thing or the event – which creates the "thing-event" *and* the immanent "sense-event" of thing or an event.'[170] This goal corresponds to the production of an 'artwork' when it 'provides the intrinsic logic of the composition of that artwork – a logic that is not separable from the knowledge of the logic of sensation, and which can only be conveyed by the knowledge of the media, materials and the elements of composition.'[171]

9. Real Convergences

The new arts/sciences research program able to deliver useful knowledge about the energy functions that simultaneously complexify and unify human and human/non-human relations is reflective. Michael Tawa has written a book about the teaching of architectural design which utilizes

---

169 Mark Burry, *Scripting Cultures: Architectural Design and Programming* (Chichester, UK: Wiley, 2011), 75.

170 Correa & Correa, 40.

171 Ibid., 40.

Involute 10, artline texta 0.4 on paper, 210 x 297 mm, September 2014. A47, 6

ana-materialistic thinking, the recovery from the materials of thinking certain immanent structures or tendencies towards higher levels of self-organization. These 'assemblages' are simultaneously associations of ideas and the 'existential infrastructure for life.' They are disposed to join together in new ways that are conducive to producing the conditions where life is lived twice, constructively and re-constructively, actively and reflectively.[172] Ana-materialistic thinking is also ana-empirical in the sense of combining observation with self-observation. It is a stance that recognizes the emotional or spiritual drama played out in the making of sense. The research program capable of conceptualizing complexity in a way likely to foster the public good balances dejection and projection, skeptical withdrawal and joyous affirmation. It is idle to imagine that a knowledge lacking these parameters can deliver anything of human interest.

According to his biographer, the great geologist James Hutton held that 'there [was] no resemblance between the world without us, and the notions that we form of it.'[173] He also allowed that 'The world... as conceived by us, is the creation of the mind itself, [it is] of the mind acted on from without, and receiving information from some external power.'[174] Thus, 'our perceptions being consistent, and regulated by uniform and constant laws, are as much realities to us, as if they were the exact copies of things really existing.'[175] But this skepticism did not produce despair: it stimulated Hutton to imagine, to look, that is, with the pattern-sensitive eye of the imagination. Playfair described Hutton's scientific genius in these terms: 'with an accurate eye for perceiving the characters of natural objects, he had in equal perfection the power of interpreting their signification, and of decyphering those ancient hieroglyphics which record

172   Tawa, *Theorising the Project*, 150ff.
173   John Playfair, 'Life of Dr Hutton', in G. W. White, ed., *James Hutton, Contributions to the History of Geology*, vol. 5 (New York: Hafner Press, 1973), 186.
174   Ibid.
175   Ibid.

the revolutions of the globe.'[176] Few mineralogists, Playfair declares, '[have] equalled him in reading the characters, which tell not only what a fossil is, but what it has been, and declare the series of changes through which it has passed.'[177] Further, 'None was more skilful in marking the gradations of nature, as she passes from one extreme to another; more diligent in observing the *continuity* [italics in original] of her proceedings, or more sagacious in tracing her footsteps, even where they were most lightly impressed.'[178]

Like Maxwell, Hutton believes in real convergences. In a version of Kant's double-aspect theory, he affirms a providential similarity between the forms of the world and the forms of the mind. Information is the outcome of a lucky synthesis of world and mind. It is the joy of recognition. Each perception of the external world 'my wandering sense entrancing,/ Tells me back my thoughts aloud,/ All the joys of Truth enhancing.' A complementarity is presumed to exist between mental and physical worlds but its demonstration is the work of sight married to insight, observation coupled with imagination. Playfair's own metaphors embody this real convergence theory. Natural objects, he writes, have 'characters.' Nature advances by 'footsteps.' Conventionally, the relationship between a character qua letter of the alphabet and its sound value is considered to be arbitrary. Letters in combination, or words, are regarded as conventional signs for concepts. In contrast, a footstep has an indexical relationship to the foot that made it. It is a trace of passage. In Playfair's figurative narrative, sign and trace are both mimetic. A primordial resemblance between the character of nature and the symbol-forming capacity of the human animal is assumed. A common movement, at once physical and intellectual, is imagined, an idea not remote from the hypothesis that 'early language was not naming in the conventional sense but representation of one kind of physical activity by means of another, displaced in time but

---

176 Ibid.
177 Ibid.
178 Ibid. For further discussion, see Carter, *Dark Writing*, 38-44.

similar in spatial relationship.'[179] The primary form of this 'primordial' communication where gesture preceded writing or speech would not be linear, the comparison of one state to another, but vortical, an involution of convergent interests. What, Paul Valéry asks in his *Philosophy of the Dance*, 'is a metaphor if not a kind of pirouette performed by an idea, enabling us to assemble its diverse names or images?'[180] 'Hamlet's Mill' might be the pirouette formed by the idea of public space when public space is designed for complexity rather than simplicity.

Here the project might rejoin concerns expressed by Lyotard. If the power to produce knowledge depends on its legitimation through institutionally mediated consensus, the opportunity to produce art can be limited by the expectation of the audience. In both cases 'there is an identical call for order, a desire for unity, for identity, for security, or popularity (in the sense of *Öffentlichkeit*, of "finding a public").'[181] The call for realism, for an identification of the real with what can be presented, effectively disavows the recognition theory of knowledge. These are matters of particular moment for design, which seeks to mediate between scientific hypothesis and artistic intuition, and which in both cases combines a paralogical skepticism about the present order with a desire to make seeming instabilities performative, generative, that is, of new orders of sociability. Realism is the price paid for delegitimizing feedback. Writing of the new global cities where no-one 'lives,' Lyotard suggests that the megalopolis, 'does not permit writing, inscribing.'[182] 'It follows that public space, *Öffentlichkeit*, in these conditions, stops being the space for experiencing, testing and affirming the state of a mind open

179 Mary LeCron Foster, 'The Symbolic Structure of Primordial Language,' in *Human Evolution: Biosocial Perspectives*, ed. S.L. Washburn and E. R. McCown (Menlo Park, Calif.: Benjamin/Cummings, 1978), 77-121.

180 Paul Valéry, 'Philosophy of the Dance,' trans. R. Manheim in *What Is Dance?: Readings in Theory and Criticism*, ed. R. Copeland and M. Cohen (New York: Oxford University Press), 65.

181 Lyotard, 'What is Postmodernism?,' 73.

182 Jean-François Lyotard, 'Time Today' in *The Inhuman: Reflections on Time*, trans. Geoffrey Bennington and Rachel Bowlby (Stanford: Stanford University Press, 1991), 76.

to the event, and in which the mind seeks to elaborate an idea of that state itself, especially under the sign of the "new." Public space today is transformed into a market of cultural commodities, in which "the new" has become an additional source of surplus-value.'[183] The 'public space' invoked here is not the *Platz* as such but the larger sphere of public interaction and includes the institutionalized spaces of public knowledge production. The question is whether the university can continue to be a space for affirming the state of mind open to an event, or whether, in the interests of marketable expertise, it refuses to admit, imagine and visualize the turbulence of change.

---

183 Ibid., 76.

Involutes

A Note on the Drawings

The drawings in *Turbulence* are graphic *involutes*. They translate into lines 'perplexed combinations of concrete objects,' to borrow Thomas de Quincey's definition.[184] They represent 'compound experiences incapable of being disentangled.' The involute is a recurring complex of ideas or as John Barrell puts it, 'an intricately coiled or interwoven manifold.'[185] Like the involuted shell (from which De Quincey borrowed his figure), it consists of overlays of later experience onto earlier experience. It describes a way of organizing experience that occurs repeatedly, a manifold to which successive associative clusters can be affixed.

A vellum palimpsest or roll of paper reused over centuries might, De Quincey reflects, well provoke mirth because of 'the grotesque collisions of those successive themes, having no natural connection, which by pure accident have consecutively occupied the roll.'[186] But, De Quincey claims, in the 'mighty palimpsest,' the 'human brain,' there cannot be such 'incoherencies':[187]

> The fleeting accidents of a man's life, and its external shows, may indeed be irrelate and incongruous; but the organizing principles which fuse into harmony, and gather about fixed predetermined centres, whatever heterogeneous elements life may have accumulated from without, will not permit the grandeur of human unity greatly to be violated.[188]

---

184 See main text, note 130.

185 Frank Kermode, *London Review of Books* 13 (9), 9 May 1991. Accessed at http://www.lrb.co.uk/v13/n09/frank-kermode/elizabeths-chamber

186 Thomas de Quincey, 'The Palimpsest of The Human Brain,' *Suspiria de Profundis*. Accessed at https://ebooks.adelaide.edu.au/d/de_quincey/thomas/suspiria-de-profundis/chapter2.html

187 Ibid.

188 Ibid.

De Quincey expresses a revolutionary or rotatory notion of ideation. Involutes, or thought forms are four dimensional objects. Drawings of them, confined to the two dimensions of the page, seek to represent these additional dimensions as an act of turning over, of condensation and extraction that can be compared to the activity of the centrifuge. The graphic involute gives epistemological value to the interference patterns that arise when the principle of involution acts to fuse the incongruous into a harmonious form. Involuted shells are types of non-linear growth; their helical expansion is a product of feedback; they model the vortical motion of turbulence, when it is understood to be the maelstrom of creativity.

Leibniz speculated, 'It seems that there is some centre of the entire universe, and some general infinite vortex... .'[189] Some shells are miniatures of this. Others depict other topologies of generation and regeneration. In his introduction to *The Conchologist's First Book*, Edgar Allan Poe describes heterostrophic shells, 'whose spires reverse; revolute, rolled backwards.'[190] In any case, like de Quincey's Dark Interpreter, the involute is a guide to the Real, a personal map in which one might successively wrap oneself, for the Interpreter as an 'apparition... but a reflex of yourself' – 'in uttering your secret feelings to him, you make this phantom the dark symbolic mirror for reflecting to the daylight what else must be hidden for ever.'[191]

This describes the motivation of these sketches. They express 'secret feelings,' a desire to weave the 'irrelate' into arrangements or shared regions. Some of the drawings dating from 2006 (Involutes 6, 8, 9 and, to a lesser extent, 7) feature chiasmatic figures, spindles, ropes or other

189 Catherine Wilson, 'Atoms, Minds, and Vortices in *De Summa Rerum*: Leibniz vis-à-vis Hobbes and Spinoza,' in *The Young Leibniz and His Philosophy*, ed. Stuart Brown (Dordrecht: Springer, 1999), 223-243.

190 Edgar Allan Poe, *The Conchologist's First Book* (Philadelphia: Haswell, Barrington, and Haswell, 1839), glossary.

191 See main text, note 134.

diagonal armatures paired with counter-patterns. But the writings in the notebooks where these were drawn offer limited insight into their purpose or meaning. Others possess a rotatory impulse, like the spreading of a wing or an archipelago (Involute 5),[192] which, in a more recent drawing (Involute 2) is elevated to the dominant organizing principle. Other later drawings (Involutes 1 and 4) spiral back to the conchological origins of the involute. All of the drawings are contemporary with public art commissions that considered the representation of turbulence, but no formal resemblance is discernible: they are not preparatory sketches, suggesting instead the turbulent supplement of ideation that exceeds representation in design.

Matter that matters is informed immanent with sociability; it exhibits, a plastic desire to recombine. Transposed to the realm of landscape design, these drawings describe ambience or atmosphere, considered as the neglected dimension of public space design. They represent processes suspended between the solid and the liquid. Like shells, which, uniquely according to Poe, mingle the organic and the inorganic, they imagine a world belonging equally to biology and geology. They are movement forms, environments considered from the point of view of passages or journeys. The passages of different, juxtaposed surfaces are not part objects in search of a lost whole form. They desire to overlap, interpenetrate and yield to the influence of the neighborhood.

Drawings like these can be used to communicate the creative potential of feedback in the emergence of designs. Even if they map to no recognizable project – failing to represent any perspectivally-consistent environment – they do have a machine-like quality, suggesting a generative rhythm or vibrational unity giving form to the 'irrelate.' Rotation or speed

---

192   References in the drawing to 'Merope,' 'the veiled one,' one of the Pleiades, or Seven Sisters
       connect this drawing to 'Golden Grove,' a public art project developed by Taylor, Cullity,
       Lethlean and Material Thinking for the Darlington Campus, University of Sydney (2006-2009).
       Seven 'nodes,' corresponding to the constellation, can be made out. (Carter, *Places Made After Their
       Stories*, 178.)

of spin is hinted at; and fields spun out of this rotation possess both a tension and a permeability, as if rates of changes modifying the pattern can produce dissolutions of surface, involuting the two dimensional plane into wormhole arabesques. Such patterns evolve but also involve, climb out of the matrix but also burrow back into it. Outward journeys are caught in the feedback of inward journeys: emergence brings us closer than ever to beginnings. As Emmanuel Levinas once wrote of a Charles Lapicque's *Figures entrelacées* (1946-1947), 'Lines rid themselves of their role as skeletons to become the infinity of all possible paths of propinquity.'[193]

---

193   Carter, *Repressed Spaces*, 192.